'THE BROONS'
DAYS OOT!

Our big project at school this year is <u>SCOTLAND</u>. We had to think up an idea about the country we live in.

I thought about all the great days we have had as a family going to see different places.

I got the whole family to help and I did lots of research at the library because I wanted everything up to date. The library lady helped too and I learned about the internet and how to look things up and print it all out.

Maw let me have some of her pictures from her memory box and I went round places getting leaflets too.

<u>Horace Broon.</u>

Very well done Horace! You have clearly done your homework – you have carried out your research well and have created a project to be proud of.

Teacher

Published 2009 by Waverley Books Ltd, David Dale House,
New Lanark, Scotland, ML11 9DJ

9 8 7 6 5 4 3 2

Waverley Books Ltd gratefully acknowledge the assistance and co-operation of The National
Trust For Scotland, Historic Scotland, Visit Scotland, and Nicolson Maps.

The special edition of The Map Of Scotland enclosed with this book is courtesy and
© 2009 Nicolson Maps, 3 Frazer Street, Largs, Ayrshire KA30 9HP, Scotland.
Further local and national maps are available from www.nicolsonmaps.com

The Broons text is by David Donaldson, The Broons scriptwriter, with additional material by
Christopher Riches and Waverley Books Ltd.

Horace Broon was assisted with design matters and layout by Hugo Breingan and by
Christopher Riches on editorial aspects.

Horace Broon wishes to thank the Teachers at Glebe Street School and the nice library lady
at Glebe Street Library, who helped with the computer and by getting some of the high-
up books down and for suggesting Trebuchet as a good 'easy-read' typeface for the main
pages.

ISBN: 978-1-902407-94-4
Printed and bound in the EU

ImpoRTinT biTs ↙

Publisher's note

For all major attractions we have provided a postcode so that you can locate the place by use of
a satnav or a computer mapping application, a telephone number for direct contact and a web
address. Where there is free admission to a particular visitor attraction, we have mentioned this.
For all other attractions listed, there is likely to be a charge and you should consult the attraction's
website or telephone for details. We suggest that you also check for details of opening times before
deciding to visit a particular place. Quite a number of attractions are closed during the winter
months, and we would not want to spoil your day oot. Whilst we made every effort to ensure that
the information was accurate at the time of compilation, we know that information can change over
time. Please let us know of any changes so that we can keep the book up to date.

We are very grateful to the many organisations and individuals for permission to reproduce
photographs and illustrations in this book. We have made every effort to contact the copyright
holders of material reproduced in this book.

For any queries or suggestions, please contact us at: Waverley Books Ltd., David Dale House,
New Lanark, Scotland ML11 9DJ.

2 Don't miss the special offers at the back o' this book, on page 144

THE BROONS'
DAYS OOT!
CONTENTS

4	Maw's Handy Hints & Picnic Tips		74	Glencoe
8	Edinburgh Castle		76	Ben Nevis
10	Edinburgh: The Royal Mile		80	The West Highland Railway
14	Edinburgh: Holyrood		84	On Skye
16	More tae do in Edinburgh		88	Loch Ness
19	The Firth of Forth		90	Urquhart Castle
22	The Royal Highland Show		92	A Day Oot Aroond Inverness
24	East Lothian		94	Birds of Scotland
26	The Borders		96	Very Old Places
28	Oor Favourite Museums		98	The Vikings
30	Dumfries and Galloway		100	The Cairngorms
32	Ayrshire		102	Camping
34	Culzean Castle		104	Highland Wildlife
36	A Day Oot wi Burns		106	Distilleries
38	On Arran		110	Royal Deeside
42	The Waverley		112	Aberdeen
44	New Lanark		114	Highland Games
46	A Day of Rural Life		117	Pitlochry and the Centre of Scotland
48	Glasgow: Kelvingrove Museum		120	Great Gardens
50	Glasgow: The Tenement House		122	Dundee
51	More tae do in Glasgow		124	Abbeys tae Visit
52	Botanic Gardens		126	Festivals
54	Glasgow: Charles Rennie Mackintosh		127	Oor Favourite Castles
56	Oor Favourite Art Galleries		130	Stirling and Roond Aboot
58	Country Parks		132	Falkirk Wheel
60	Loch Lomond		134	Blair Drummond Safari Park
62	When it's Wet		136	The East Neuk
64	Inveraray		138	St Andrews
66	Loch Awe and Oban		140	On the Beach
68	On Mull		142	Horace's Really Useful Index
70	On Iona		144	Special Offers
72	To the Islands			

Kids go FREE!

3

Maw's Handy Hints & Picnic Tips

HANDY HINTS

Don't forget the Map!
There's nothing worse than guessin' which way to go, and make sure everyone
agrees about where we're going, before we go.

What to Wear!! – Our lot take ages deciding what to wear. It's not easy, but you
need to persuade folk to be comfy, and if there's walking to be done, Daphne's high
heels are not allowed.

Spare Stuff – it's guaranteed if there is a loch or a burn within a mile, one of our lot
will get wet, so there's usually some spare pants and socks in a bag.

Sun Hats for the Bairn and the Twins - make sure Paw and Granpaw have their big
hankies to put knots in at the corners. Long-sleeved T-shirts are also a great idea
for a long day in the sun.

Waterproofs that scrunch up wee are great for that unexpected shower and are
great for keeping the wind off too.

First Aid Kit - just a wee one with a few plasters and antiseptic wipes can make all
the difference. It's really just a case of which of the Twins or the Bairn falls over
first and scrapes a knee.

Sun Lotion - a must for the wee ones particularly if you are out and about. Mad Dogs
and Englishmen are not the only ones oot in the midday sun! And Midge Repellent.

Travel Sickness - take sealable plastic bags. There's always a use for plastic bags.
If you've got a family member that doesn't travel well, ask your pharmacist about
some Travel Sickness pills.

Toys to keep the bairns quiet on the way - avoid games and toys that make heid-
splittin' noises and things that are liable to damage clothes and seats, such as felt-
tip pens and plasticine, and puzzles that'll drive folk daft if a piece goes missing.

Nibbles and Snacks - take some that won't do damage to clothes and surroundings
when scoffed on the way. Raisins and apples?

A wee sewing kit can be handy, just for any running repairs to breeks' buttons, and
Joe always has his penknife wi' a' the gadgets.

For big games - a bat and ball or a Frisbee and a beach ball or a football. And
whatever you do, don't forget a bucket and spade if you are going to the beach.
Don't forget your purse or your wallet, but take care of it at all times.

And don't forget to put everything off and lock up when you leave the hoose. Doors
and windows!

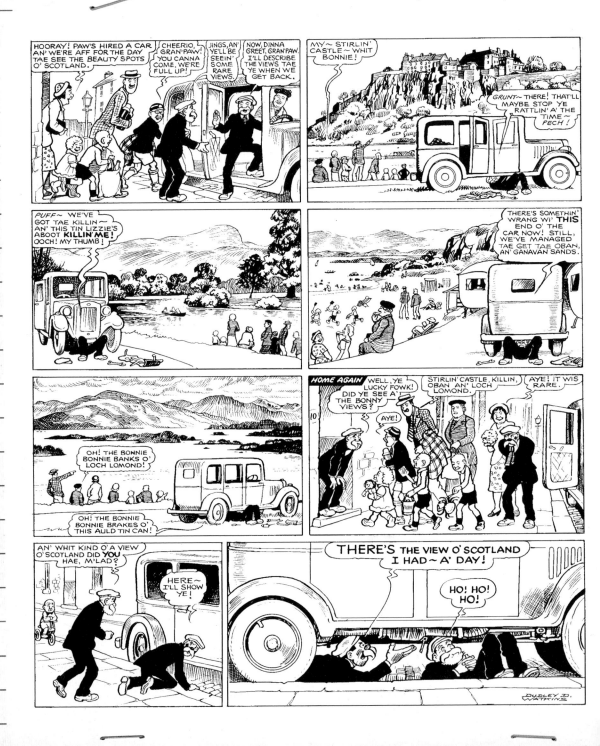

Mair Handy Hints & Picnic Tips

THE PICNIC

For us, often the picnic is not the be all and end all – but when we go to a Games mebbe - if you rely on the food at the stalls it can get awfy expensive wi' eleven mouths to feed! A picnic's the very dab.

Keep all the picnic things together so you don't need to waste half a day hunting for stuff.

We've got a big <u>picnic basket</u> - Paw added an assortment of straps and old belts that hold everything in place, and there's a handle at each end so two folk can carry it, and the menfolk (except one) all take turns.

<u>Rugs, and an old tablecloth</u> , and if the ground is likely to be wet, you'll need a groundsheet or a big polythene sheet - like Hen uses for the decoratin'. Also folding chairs to sit on.

We've got some of these boxes with press-on lids that are really handy, but best pack your sandwiches in greaseproof paper so they don't go soggy.

<u>Have plenty to drink</u>. Take three times as much drink as you think you will need as you never have enough.

<u>Cutlery</u> - even if you're planning on having finger food, you may still need a spare knife and wee spoons for yogurts.

<u>Take a cutting board</u> and two sharp knives - a bread knife and a wee knife to cut fruit and veg. Also a tin opener.

Don't forget the <u>Thermos</u> of tea or coffee or soup - Paw likes something to keep him warm!

<u>Firelighters</u> if you're going to make a real fire, the barbecue bits and pieces, the big fork and fish-slice and the camping stove.

<u>Food Safety</u> - Remember that picnics can be the cause of food poisoning if you don't take care: nasty bugs love picnic food left out in the sun. So - keep your food cool in the <u>coolbox</u>. It's really important to keep your meat cold.

<u>Have a grand day oot!</u>
Maw

Loads o' summer picnic an' barbecue recipes in Maw's 'But An' Ben' Cookbook — It's in the shops now!

7

Edinburgh Castle

(i)

Edinburgh Castle EH1 2NG
Tel: 0131 225 9846
www.edinburghcastle.gov.uk

EDINBURGH CASTLE
by The Broons "Royal" Family

Paw Broon

EDINBURGH CASTLE Scotland's number 1 tourist attraction! If ye want tae walk in the footsteps of just aboot onybody that's a famous Scot, then this is the place tae dae it. Ye'll be walking with a' the famous folk of history . . . except maybe Bonnie Prince Charlie. They widnae let him in.

The approach tae the castle is across the esplanade where the world-famous MILITARY TATTOO is held every year. But ye'll need tae book early tae get tickets for this if ye want tae see it. Once across the castle esplanade, it's onward over the impressive drawbridge and ye've stormed the castle! The only "sojers" that micht bar yer entry these days are the staff if ye've no' bought yer ticket at the office. The castle isnae impregnable now, but ye'll still need guid legs tae get up an' doon a' the cobbles an' stairs.

Granpaw Broon

Ye mustn't miss the statue of Field Marshal Earl Haig on his horse on the esplanade. Douglas Haig was the Scot who was the commander of the British forces in the First World War. Bein' an auld veteran masel', the REAL Old Contemptible, as Maw calls me, I aye have tae stop an' salute The Chief.

Hen Broon

The first thing ye see when ye get up intae the castle is the view!! And ye can see why the castle was easy to defend. It sits on its craggy rock and ye can see for miles. It widna hae been easy tae sneak up on the sojers un-noticed. There's been a fort of sorts on this Edinburgh Rock for 3,000 years.

Try and be at the castle at one o'clock. There's been a gun fired here at this time since 1861 and it still makes you jump if you're not expecting it. It's called "THE ONE O'CLOCK GUN". There's always a big crowd gathered about at one, with their hands to their ears. Oor Bairn got a right scare and near jumped out of her nappy.

The Bairn

The Bairn said she was only pretendin tae greet
She said she kent the gun was goin' boom!
She only was greetin' tae get a big ice cream at the shop.

8

N.B.R. Local Charge 1/6
ONE BICYCLE (Accompanied by Passenger
At Company's Limited risk
EDINBURGH Way. Stn. (No. 1
To
DUNDEE (Tay Bridge)
via The Forth Bridge and Cupar
This Ticket which is available for a single
Journey only, must be given up at death
Station. For Conditions SEE BACK.

Days Out:
Edinburgh Castle

THE STONE OF DESTINY is the original stone that Scottish Monarchs were crowned on. It was taken from Scone Palace by King Edward I of England in 1296 to Westminster Abbey in London, where English monarchs sat on it for 700 years.

In 1996 it was returned to Scotland by Her Majesty Queen Elizabeth.

St Margaret's Chapel sits near the top of the castle rock. It was built by St Margaret's son King David about the year 1130, and is the oldest building in Edinburgh.

The Crown Room of the Royal Palace contains the crown jewels of Scotland (called "The Honours of Scotland") - the crown, the sceptre and the sword, all about five hundred years old. They were used at the coronation of Mary Queen of Scots in 1543.

The National War Memorial was opened at the castle in July 1927 by the Prince of Wales and Field Marshal Earl Haig. It's a very quiet place and it makes you think.

THE
EDINBURGH
MILITARY
TATTOO
1963

A.E. MASWELL MILLER
1963

BOOm!

ⓘ
Edinburgh Military Tattoo
Tel: 0131 225 1188
www.edintattoo.co.uk

9

Edinburgh: The Royal Mile

ⓘ The Scotch Whisky Experience
EH1 2NE.
Tel: 0131 220 0441
www.whisky-heritage.co.uk

STEPPIN' OOT DOON THE ROYAL MILE
by The Broons "Royal" Family

Maw Broon
We're a' writing this doon in oor family diary as we step oot DOON the Royal Mile in Edinburgh. We're haein' a wee flask on the Castle Esplanade afore we set aff for oor day. It mak's real sense tae "do" the mile goin' doonhill. Wid ye no' agree? And wid ye believe it, ane o' Edinburgh's traffic wardens is already booking folks' cars and it's no' yet nine o'clock. Come wi' the train!!

Joe Broon
Exactly 57 steps take us fae the wee sentry kiosk at the exit o' the esplanade past the CAMERA OBSCURA tae the SCOTCH WHISKY EXPERIENCE visitor attraction. Nae further explanation required. In we go! Had tae keep Granpaw in check here. Ootside again, it's only 110 gentle strides mair tae reach THE HUB, Edinburgh's Festival Centre. It's in an auld converted kirk. Pit ae foot in front o' anither 18 times fae here and ye're passin' the ENSIGN EWART pub. Ensign Charles Ewart was the famous Scots Grey wha captured the French standard at the Battle of Waterloo. There's a memorial tae him back up on the Castle Esplanade. The captured eagle standard is in the castle.

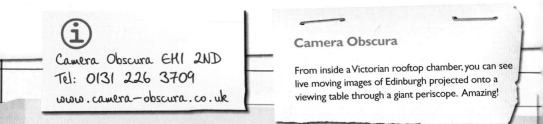

ⓘ Camera Obscura EH1 2ND
Tel: 0131 226 3709
www.camera-obscura.co.uk

Camera Obscura

From inside a Victorian rooftop chamber, you can see live moving images of Edinburgh projected onto a viewing table through a giant periscope. Amazing!

Daphne Broon
It's 140 paces now, doon tae the North Bridge crossroads and ye pass mair woollen and tartan shops than even I can visit. Kilts, skirts, tartan souvenirs, jumpers, cashmeres, Jimmy hats and anything ye can think o' that visitors like. On yer left at North Bridge there's DEACON BRODIE'S pub. Brodie was the 18th-century rogue said to hae been the inspiration for Robert Louis Stevenson's "Dr Jekyll and Mr Hyde". Jist behind is the WRITERS' MUSEUM in Lady Stair's Close.

Ye jist must mak' a diversion here an' turn right alang North Bridge til ye see the statue o' wee GREYFRIARS BOBBY. He was the Skye Terrier that guarded the grave o' his master John Gray in Greyfriars Cemetery for years. The story was made intae a Walt Disney film. Back at the crossroads it's 98 steps tae the HEART O' MIDLOTHIAN. It's laid oot in cobbles richt beside ST GILES KIRK. Ye've a problem here . . . dae ye visit St Giles or the ROYAL MILE WHISKIES shop across the road? Go tae baith. We did.

Hen Broon

I hae tae count everybody else's steps cos I only tak' half as many. 114 easy strides and we're doon at <u>MERCAT CROSS</u> opposite City Chambers. It's a kick-off point for guided walking tours tae auld underground streets and ghost tours. They're great fun, especially if ye hae a lassie wi' ye that needs a wee cuddle in the dark. 20 more steps now and we're passing the statue o' <u>ADAM SMITH</u>, the lad that wrote "The Wealth of Nations". I wonder what he'd say aboot a' the bank disasters here of late? Or maybe he'd change his book tae "The Debts of Nations". Time for me to stride on doon tae South Bridge at <u>THE TRON</u>. Maggie tells me it was 150 paces fae Adam Smith on his plinth. Lots o' shops and cafes aboot here.

St Giles.

(i)

St Giles Cathedral EH1 1RE.
Tel: 0131 225 9442
www.stgilescathedral.org.uk FREE
Royal Mile Whiskies EH1 1PW.
Tel: 0131 524 9380
www.royalmilewhiskies.com

(i)

The Writers' Museum EH1 2PA
Tel: 0131 529 4901
www.cac.org.uk FREE
Greyfriars Kirk EH1 2QQ.
Tel: 0131 226 5429
www.greyfriarskirk.com FREE

ADAM SMITH

Visit The
Scotch Whisky
Visitor Experience

NEXT TO EDINBURGH CAS

ENJOY AN EXCITING JOURN
DISCOVERY THROUGH
THE STORY OF SCOTCH WH

THE
MAKING
THE SMEL
THE TAST
THE SECRETS
DISCOVER

(i)
The Museum of Childhood
EH1 1TG. Tel: 0131 529 414
www.cac.org.uk   FREE

Maw Broon
175 paces in ma guid shoes past pubs and folk eatin' an' shoppin' till we arrive at the <u>MUSEUM OF CHILDHOOD</u>. The Bairn is fair lookin' forward tae this as she's ta'en three times as many steps as the rest o' us wi' her wee leggies, the wee lamb. Opposite is the <u>BRASS RUBBING CENTRE</u>.

We're fair birlin' doon the High Street now and left, right, left, right 42 times and we're at <u>JOHN KNOX'S HOUSE</u>. It's a lovely auld building an' worth a nosey inside. Ootside there's a lump o' a thing ca'd the Netherbow Wellhead, a relic fae 1675 o' the drinking water system o' auld Edinburgh, "Auld Reekie" as my father kent it. 28 strides mair and it's the <u>SCOTTISH STORYTELLING CENTRE</u> next. I have tae say there's nae end o' things in this street.

Horace Broon
This counting steps is getting silly, but I have tae join in. 48 steps now and we've arrived at the World's End crossroads. At the Battle of Flodden in 1513, King James IV and maist o' the nobles o' Scotland and hunners o' Scottish fighting men ("the flowers o' the forest") were slaughtered. Folk thought it was the end o' the world and hastily built a wall roond Edinburgh Toon tae protect it. The <u>WORLD'S END</u> pub on the corner is built on the foundations of the old wall.

Maw

(i)
Brass Rubbing Centre
EH1 1SS.
Tel: 0131 556 4364
www.cac.org.uk   FREE

(i)
John Knox House and Scottish
Storytelling Centre EH1 1SR.
Tel: 0131 556 9579
www.scottishstorytellingcentre.co.uk

John Knox's house.

Granpaw

Aff we go again, me oot in front. The Royal Mile is ca'd the Canongate now and it's quieter doon here, an' I'm showing the family a clean pair o' heels as I canter through 320 steps (there's nae haudin' me back here!) to the green-and-white frontage o' ma favourite shop, CADENHEAD'S WHISKY SHOP. I've been in twa whisky shops already the day and it's third time lucky for me. A rare cask-strength Ardbeg stowed awa' in ma jaicket afore ye can say "Jings, Crivvens, Help ma Bob". 42 strides tak's me tae the CANONGATE TOLBOOTH as the family catch up.

We're a' together again for 52 mair steps tae the CANONGATE KIRK. Edinburgh's past celebrities are buried in the graveyard here, including "Clarinda" (Mrs MacLehose), described as the "sweetheart of Robert Burns". ANE o' his sweethearts I'd say. It's a fair bet Rabbie had a rare time o' it, up and doon this street in his day. There's a statue of poet ROBERT FERGUSSON by sculptor David Annand on the pavement here. Fergusson was much admired by Rabbie Burns. The puir lad died aged 24 in the Bedlam Asylum.

Maggie Broon

Time tae call a halt for the day and it's only 190 steps tae CLARINDA'S TEAROOM. An Edinburgh institution and a welcome ane at that for us . . . tea time. Ye'll be hard pushed tae find better hame cookin' in Edinburgh. It's usually busy, an' it certainly was when oor gang descended upon them. What a rare end tae a rare day oot in the Capital. Cheers, everybody!

The Twins

We coonted the day as 1,410 steps fae the Castle tae here. There's still a wee bit tae the Parliament at the bottom o' the street, but we'll go there anither day. We're no' movin'.

Edinburgh Rock
Made in Scotland

(i) Cadenhead's Whisky Shop
EH8 8BN.
Tel: 0131 536 5864
http://edinburgh.wmcadenhead.com
Clarinda's Tearoom EH8 8BS.
Tel: 0131 557 1888

(i) The People's Story,
Canongate Tolbooth
EH8 8BN.
Tel: 0131 529 4057
www.cac.org.uk FREE

Edinburgh: Holyrood

AT THE BOTTOM O' THE HIGH STREET
by Maggie Broon

Maggie

Sometimes it's hard for me tae tear masel' away fae the braw shops in Edinburgh, but there are some things that just can't be missed . . . like oor new Parliament building, its Royal neighbour Holyrood Palace and Arthur's Seat, which for me is a funny name for a hill. First stop just has tae be the <u>PALACE OF HOLYROODHOUSE</u>.

And it's only a hop an' skip ower the road tae the next <u>FREE</u> port of call, the new <u>SCOTTISH PARLIAMENT</u> building. Me and Daphne thought it looked real cool, but Granpaw and Paw thought it looked like a pund o' mince. Whatever ye think o' it, it's oor Parliament and it's worth a look.

Efter a' the politics and intrigue o' "The Holyroods" ye'll be raring for a bit o' fresh air and Edinburgh's rightly popular Arthur's Seat is jist across the road. <u>ARTHUR'S SEAT</u> is the main peak o' a wee group o' hills right in the middle o' the city in Holyrood Park. The hill itsel' is aboot 823 ft high. It's an extinct volcano aboot 350 million years old. I'm aye suspicious o' "extinct" volcanos, but if this ane erupts when ye're here on yer day oot, ye'd hae tae say ye've been awfy unlucky. There are so many different ways tae reach the top, the best advice is jist tae pick oot ony path and follow it. If it's still goin' up, ye've no' reached the summit . . . keep walkin'! Local tip is that the easiest way up is fae Dunsapie Loch on the wee road that goes richt roond the hill.

Here's a guid wee tip tae end yer day oot here. Jist east o' Holyrood Palace at the foot o' the hills ye can tak' <u>YOUR</u> seat, no' Arthur's, and watch the maist overfed swans in Scotland glidin' aboot on a wee loch. Awfy bonnie.

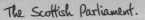
The Scottish Parliament.

Holyrood Park EH8 8HG.
Tel: 0131 652 8150
(Rangers)
www.historic-scotland.gov.uk

Days Out: *Holyrood*

THE PALACE OF HOLYROODHOUSE

It's right at the very bottom of The Royal Mile and is Her Majesty the Queen's official residence in Scotland. Originally the site of an abbey founded by King David I in 1128 (the ruins of which are attached to the palace), the building of the palace started around 1500. The oldest surviving section is the north-west tower. The Palace has been associated with Mary Queen of Scots more than any other monarch. It was in the tower, in one of Mary Queen of Scots "private rooms" that her jealous second husband, Lord Darnley, murdered Mary's Italian secretary, Rizzio (for a long time afterwards people said that blood stains could still be seen on the floor). Charles II had built most of the palace we see today. The work was finished in the 1670s, but he never visited it. Bonnie Prince Charlie stayed here briefly in 1745, when the soldiers at the castle refused to let him in.

The Queen has a big garden party here every year, when people who have done good work are invited. About 8,000 people come and they work their way through 27,000 cups of tea, 20,000 sandwiches and 20,000 slices of cake!

THE SCOTTISH PARLIAMENT

This is called Holyrood as well, but it's no Palace. Probably the costliest building of recent times, it is certainly one of those buildings that you either love or hate. You can hear the Scottish government in action in the debating chamber if you are lucky. On non-parliament-business days, staff are about to answer questions. Created by world-famous architect Enric Miralles, the design is supposed to look like upturned boats on a shore. It's not really one building but a collection of buildings. And whatever you think of it, it's not like anything else you will have ever seen.

Palace of Holyroodhouse,
EH8 8DX.
Tel: 0131 556 5100
www.royalcollection.org.uk

The Scottish Parliament
EH99 1SP. FREE
Tel: 0131 348 5200
www.scottish.parliament.uk

More tae do in Edinburgh

There are hunners o' things tae do in Edinburgh, but ye'd expect that seeing as it is a UNESCO City o' Literature and a World Heritage Site and is known as the Athens o' the North.

THE ROYAL YACHT BRITANNIA
OCEAN TERMINAL, EDINBURGH
2009

The Royal Yacht Britannia
EH6 6JJ. Tel: 0131 555 5566
www.royalyachtbritannia.co.uk
Edinburgh Zoo EH12 6TS.
Tel: 0131 334 9171
www.edinburghzoo.org.uk
Rosslyn Chapel EH25 9PU.
Tel: 0131 440 2159
www.rosslynchapel.org.uk

Royal Yacht Britannia

Once it was used by the Queen and the Royal family as a floating palace to travel the around the world. Now it is moored at the Ocean Terminal in Leith, just to the north of the centre of Edinburgh and you can make a royal tour of the boat.

Edinburgh Zoo

Edinburgh Zoo is the largest and most exciting wildlife attraction in Scotland, committed to the highest standards of animal welfare, conservation and environmental education. In just one day, you can meet over 1,000 wonderful animals in a beautiful parkland setting on the outskirts of Edinburgh. There are some wonderful attractions for you to experience, plus you can also enjoy a wide range of visitor facilities and masses of events and activities throughout the year.

Rosslyn Chapel

This church, a few miles south of Edinburgh at Roslin, was founded in 1446 by William St Clair, the third and last Prince of Orkney, and is noted for its lack of conformity with fashion or contemporary architecture. The church has a wealth of carvings, including the Apprentice Pillar. In the carvings there are references to the Knights Templar, Biblical stories, pagan symbols and the largest number of 'green men' that have ever be found in a medieval building. There are also carvings of plants from the New World, which are said to have been carved before Columbus discovered it. It played an important role in the book *The Da Vinci Code* and is one of the strangest buildings you will ever visit.

CITY OF LITERATURE

Edinburgh is the world's first UNESCO City of Literature, a pioneer in a new international network of creative cities.

The Edinburgh UNESCO City of Literature Trust was established to promote book culture in Edinburgh, encourage involvement with Scotland's literature and develop literary partnerships around the world.

edinburgh
(edɪnbʌrə) *n.*
UNESCO City of
Literature

Find out what else is going on in literary Edinburgh.
Visit www.cityofliterature.com

17

NELSON MONUMENT

The Best Views of Edinburgh from 2 Historic Landmarks

SCOTT MONUMENT

The Best Views of Edinburgh from 2 Historic Landmarks

Places to see the view

Scott Monument

This monument, containing a marble statue of the novelist Sir Walter Scott was completed in 1844. It stands 200 ft high and is a confection of neo-Gothic spires, crockets, gargoyles and niches, looking like a medieval rocket. The monument has many statues of characters from Scott's novels, including Rob Roy, Ivanhoe and John Knox. There are 287 steps to the top. Climb up the internal stairway for fantastic views from the heart of Edinburgh's historic Old and New Towns and over Princes Street Gardens which provide a beautiful green island between the two.

Calton Hill

Perched high on Calton Hill in the heart of Edinburgh sits a monument to Admiral Lord Nelson, and it looks like an up-turned telescope! The top of the monument is the best place to experience breathtaking views of Edinburgh's Old and New Towns, Arthur's Seat and the distant Forth rail and road bridges. There are other monuments on Calton Hill as well. The strangest is the National Monument, originally designed to be like the Parthenon in Athens, only the money ran out and just twelve columns were built – less a National Monument, more Edinburgh's Folly. It was meant to be a monument to those who died in the Napoleonic Wars.

Museums and Art Galleries

There are lots of Museums and Art Galleries in Edinburgh, especially the National Gallery of Scotland and the National Museum of Scotland. They may be museums full of old things but they do keep changing. The National Portrait Gallery is completely closed until 2012 and the old part of the National Museum of Scotland is closed until 2011 while they are refurbished.

The Georgian House

Find out what is was like to live in Edinburgh's New Town – an inspired creation of sweeping crescents, broad streets and gracious squares. It offered wealthy citizens in the late 18th century a means of escape from the overcrowded tenements of the Old Town, around the Royal Mile. The Georgian House, with its elegant furnished interior, is located at No. 7 Charlotte Square. The Square was conceived by the architect Robert Adam as a vision of the Georgian ideal in the centre of Edinburgh. The Georgian House has been magnificently restored to show a typical Edinburgh New Town house of the late 18th and early 19th century. The fine collection of period furniture, porcelain, silver and glass, reflect the lifestyle and social and economic conditions of the time. The house also features the 'Below Stairs' life of the servants who made the elegant lifestyle possible.

(i)

The Scott Monument and the Nelson Monument
www.edinburgh.gov.uk/monuments
The Georgian House EH2 4DR.
Tel: 0844 493 2118
www.nts.org.uk

The Firth of Forth

FACT FILE

FORTH RAIL BRIDGE

- The first proposed railway bridge was designed by Thomas Bouch and was to be a suspension bridge. Work was stopped when his other bridge, the Tay Bridge, collapsed.
- The present bridge was designed by John Fowler and Benjamin Baker.
- Building commenced in 1883 and it took 7 years to build. It opened on 4 March 1890.
- It was the first major bridge in the world to be made of steel.
- It is 1.5 miles long. The two main spans are each 1,710 ft long.
- It used 54,000 tons of steel.
- The railway line is 158 ft above the Forth.
- 6,500,000 rivets were used in its construction.
- There are 45 acres of metal surface to paint. The new paint being used today should last 25 years.
- Nearly 200 trains cross the bridge every day.
- It cost around £3.2 million (about £235 million at today's prices).

FORTH ROAD BRIDGE

- It was opened on 4 September 1964. It was the longest suspension bridge in Europe when it opened.
- The same company, Sir William Arrol & Co., built both the rail and the road bridges.
- It is 1.5 miles long. The central span is 3,298 ft.
- It used 39,000 tons of steel.
- The suspension cable is 2 ft in diameter and contains 11,618 individual wires.
- It cost £19.5 million (around £250 million at today's prices).
- A second Forth Road Bridge is planned for 2016.

DEEP SEA WORLD
Scotland's Shark capital

ADVENTURE COVE KIDS PLAY AREA
NEW!

Celebrate
'ear of the Frog'
with us!

(i) For information about the bridges:
www.forthbridges.org.uk
Deep Sea World KY11 1JR
Tel: 01383 411880
www.deepseaworld.com

Paw

THE FIRTH OF FORTH
by Paw Broon

The most photographed bridge in the world, I reckon. Certainly, ye'd be hard pushed tae find somebody that disnae recognise it, the world-famous <u>FORTH RAIL BRIDGE</u>, a colossal and beautiful monument tae Victorian engineering.

But afore I go on aboot the bonnie bridge, I must tell you aboot the place on the north side of the River Forth that the bairns jist love tae visit. The <u>DEEP SEA WORLD</u>. It's aboot 20 minutes in a car fae Edinburgh. But ye wid surely want tae come here on the train and cross the Forth Rail Bridge itself, unless ye're comin' fae Dundee, that is, when ye need tae get aff AFORE ye cross. Clear?

Deep Sea World is doon fae North Queensferry station (steep doon!) and it nestles richt under the mighty bridge. It jist towers ower the sealife centre like a giant red spider wi' a' its girders. It's "awesome", as the bairns put it. But, aboot the Deep Sea World. It's got the largest collection of Sand Tiger Sharks in Europe and Conger Eels and Stingrays (if that lot got oot, I wouldna fancy Aberdour beach's chances o' stayin' in the Blue Flag safe beach list!!). There's also thoosands o' weird and wonderful sea creatures tae look at through the glass. And ye can even watch divers feeding the sharks by hand. Gies me the heebie-jeebies, but the bairns loved every minute. Here's anither thing. If ye want tae jump intae a tank full o' sharks, ye can dae just that here. I kid ye not. If ye're no' feart, ye can get full training and a' the necessary equipment, and in ye go! Can ye believe it?? I'd want a suit of armour and my ain cage. I'll stick tae watchin' the sharkies through the glass.

Back oot under the bridge now in North Queensferry. It's a bonnie wee place itsel' an' there's a wee cafe richt doon there that I aye visit. Their home baking is braw.

Then it's on the train for us and over tae South Queensferry or Dalmeny as the station's ca'd. Back doon the path tae the famous <u>HAWES INN</u> under the south side o' the bridge. This inn featured in Robert Louis Stevenson's "Kidnapped". Ye can get boats here oot tae the islands in the Firth itsel'. . . and ye can watch the big boats heading doon the river. Try and come back at nicht if ye can and see the bridge a' lit up. It's like a big Christmas Tree!

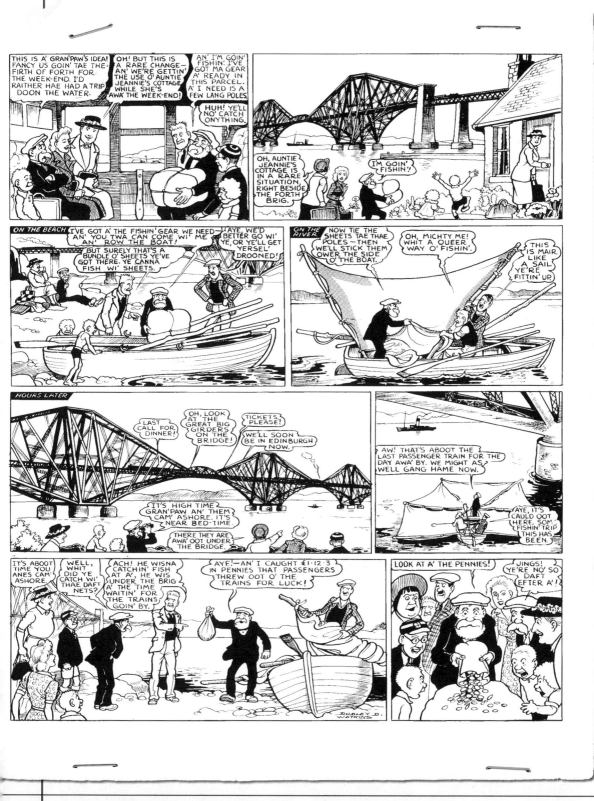

21

The Royal Highland Show

THE ROYAL HIGHLAND SHOW
by Maw Broon

This is a <u>REAL</u> day oot. I never miss it. I don't think any o' the family would willingly miss a day oot at the fair. This is <u>THE</u> show, where there honestly is something for everybody. The first show was held on the site near Holyrood Palace now occupied by the new Parliament building. Some wid argue that the smell o' "horse manure" lingers to this very day!! For many years, the show travelled around from one place to another but since aboot 1960 it's been near Edinburgh.

I'm told there are generally aboot 4,000 animals at the show in various classes and competitions. The Twins and the Bairn jist canna get enough o' things like sheep shearing, show jumpin' an' things like bees and what they dae . . . an' we never miss the Scottish Wildlife Trust stand wi' help on how tae look efter the birds in yer garden. Granpaw and Paw like tae get dressed up in their tweed suits and wander roond lookin' like gentlemen farmers.

Ye'll see horses fae Shetland ponies tae Clydesdales, falconry displays, ferrets, sheepdog trials and fly fishin' exhibitions (oor twa auld rogues are richt "fly" fishers). Then there's things like how tae mak' bagpipes, drystane dyking, basket weaving and . . . och, I could go on a' day.

And it's no' just a' farmin' stuff like coos an' ducks either . . . there's <u>FABULOUS</u> food an' drink. Jist ask oor Daphne, if ye can catch her withoot something in her moo'. There's aye plenty o' stuff tae taste, smoked salmon and shortie bein' my favourites. Daph says it's "taste and tipple", that's taste for Daphne and tipple for oor lads. There's whisky and beer and wines, sometimes mair like the New Year than June. Musical entertainment as weel, bagpipe bands of course, but pop bands, ceilidh bands, Jazz and somethin' ca'd Salsa. I love lookin' at the arts and crafts, the jewellery, the ceramics, the handmade bags, cashmere, tweeds, tartans, outdoor clothing. Jings, I canna wait tae get there again.

When oor lads are no' in the beer tents, ye'll maist likely find them at the biggest outdoor motor show in Scotland. There's everything fae the latest motor car tae bewilderin' displays o' modern farm machinery, tractors, harvesters an' things that look mair like science fiction than tattie howkin'. It's a' changed since my schooldays at the tattie-howkin' holidays.

ⓘ

Royal Highland Show
EH28 8NB.
Tel: 0131 335 6200
www.royalhighlandshow.org

Out & About: *The Royal Highland Show*

- **Where:** The Ingliston showground, eight miles west of Edinburgh, near the airport.
- **How to get there:** The entrance to the showground is off the main A8 dual carriageway in the direction of Edinburgh. It is a busy road used by people working in Edinburgh and going to the airport, so leave plenty of time in case of traffic jams.
- **When:** The show is held on Thursday to Sunday towards the end of June: 25-28 June in 2009 and 24-27 June in 2010.
- **Car parking:** There is space for 25,000 vehicles on 150 acres of land – Scotland's biggest car park.
- **Attendance:** On average over 150,000 people visit over the four days of the show.

23

East Lothian

There's lots tae do in East Lothian. My favourite is the Museum o' Flight at East Fortune. There are real planes tae see, including "Concorde" and what a sight it makes. Here's some information aboot things ye can do.

The Scottish Mining Museum

Housed in the former Lady Victoria Colliery at Newtongrange, you can find out all about the mining of coal and what it was like to be a miner – there is even a recreated roadway and coalface to give you a feeling of what it would have been like underground in the mine when it was working.

THE SCOTTISH MINING MUSEUM

NEWTONGRANGE

SCOTLAND'S BLACK DIAMONDS
SCOTTISH MINING MUSEUM

£1 off guidebook see inside

TREASURED PLACES
Scotland's favourite archive images

Scottish TOURIST BOARD
★★★★
VISITOR ATTRACTION

www.scottishminingmuseum.com

Lady Victoria Colliery see www.treasuredplaces.org.uk

National Museum of Flight East Fortune

EAST FORTUNE played an important role as an airfield during two World Wars. Now the National Museum of Flight hangars are packed with aircraft that reveal how flight developed from the Wright brothers to Concorde. The East Fortune site itself is steeped in history. In 1919 the R34 Airship took off from East Fortune to make the first east–west transatlantic flight. Now, Hangar 4 is home to Concorde G-BOAA, the first of the British Airways Concorde fleet to fly commercially. You can visit the "Concorde Experience" and follow the story of supersonic passenger flight. The other hangars display lots of civil and military aircraft, including a Spitfire and a rocket-powered Messerschmitt Me 163 Komet from the Second World War and some Scottish-made planes.

Concorde Facts

- Only twenty Concordes were ever built.
- The pointed nose helped Concorde speed through the air. It was tilted down at take-off and landing to allow the pilots to see the runway.
- Concorde used a staggering 5,637 gallons of fuel per hour.
- The top speed Concorde achieved was 1,490 miles per hour.
- There have been more US astronauts than British Airways Concorde pilots.
- Concorde carried 100 passengers and 2.5 tons of cargo.
- The standard return fare from London to New York was £6,636.

National Museum of Flight
EH39 5LF.
Tel: 0131 247 4238
www.nms.ac.uk/flight
Scottish Mining Museum
EH22 4QN.
Tel: 0131 663 7519
www.scottishminingmuseum.com

The Scottish Seabird Centre
North Berwick

THE CENTRE sits on a rocky outcrop at North Berwick Harbour, overlooking the islands of the Firth of Forth and sandy beaches of East Lothian. It has live cameras on the Bass Rock and other islands in the Firth and you can remotely watch the birds, zooming in to see the tiniest details (like the ID ring on a bird's foot), and observe thousands of nesting seabirds and marine mammals, without disturbing them in any way. The Centre also contains interactive displays and a Kid's Zone. It organises Guided bird walks along the beach and boat trips around the islands, giving you a chance to get close to the Bass Rock.

Tantallon Castle EH39 5PN
Tel: 01620 892727
www.historic-scotland.gov.uk
Dirleton Castle EH39 5ER
Tel: 01620 850330
www.historic-scotland.gov.uk
The Scottish Seabird Centre
EH39 4SS.
Tel: 01620 890202
www.seabird.org

Bass Rock

Off the coast by North Berwick is an enormous lump of rock – the Bass Rock. It is rises steeply out of the sea to reach the height of 350 ft and is a volcanic plug (like the rock Edinburgh Castle sits on). It is now home to over 100,000 gannets, our largest seabird, with a wingspan of around 6 ft, and lots of other seabirds. It was once used by the Christian hermit, St Baldred, in the 8th century and as a prison for religious and political prisoners in the 17th century. Some Jacobite prisoners in 1691 captured the Rock from their guards and held it for four years, supported by the French and resisting all attempts to recapture it. They settled on 'most honourable terms' in 1694. In *Catriona*, Robert Louis Stevenson's sequel to *Kidnapped*, David Balfour is imprisoned on the Bass Rock. ("*It was an unco place by night, unco by day; and there were unco sounds; of the calling of the solans [another name for gannets], and the plash of the sea, and the rock echoes that hung continually in our ears.*")

Gannet on Bass Rock.

Tantallon Castle

Mighty Tantallon Castle was built in the 1350s by the Earl of Douglas. In the 1380s the house of Douglas split into two branches, known as the 'Black' and the 'Red'. Tantallon passed to the junior line, the 'Red Douglases', Earls of Angus. For the next 300 years, the Earls of Angus held sway at the castle, acting out their role as one of the most powerful baronial families in Scotland. During that time it endured three great sieges, in 1491, 1528 and 1651. The last, by Oliver Cromwell's army, resulted in such devastating destruction that the mighty medieval fortress was abandoned to the birds.

Tantallon was the last truly great castle built in Scotland. This remarkable fortification is built on a promontory looking out to the Bass Rock and has earthwork defences and a massive 14th-century curtain wall with three towers in which the mighty Earls of Angus and their henchmen lived. The castle was further strengthened during the 16th century to try and protect it from the new weapon of the day – the cannon. it could not resist Cromwell's attack, however.

Dirleton Castle

Dirleton Castle has graced the heart of Dirleton since the 13th century. The impressive cluster of towers – including the imposing keep at the south-west corner – is among the oldest castle architecture surviving in Scotland. The castle suffered badly during the Wars of Independence with England that erupted in 1296.

Dirleton was captured in 1298, on the specific orders of King Edward I of England, "the Hammer of the Scots". By 1356 Dirleton had a new lord, John Haliburton. He rebuilt the battered castle, adding a new residential tower and great hall along the east side of the courtyard. Although largely ruined, the surviving storage cellars, family chapel and grim pit-prison convey a wonderful impression of lordly life in the later Middle Ages. Further buildings were added in the 16th century. The siege by Oliver Cromwell's soldiers in 1650 rendered it militarily unserviceable.

The wonderful castle gardens date from the late 19th and early 20th centuries.

ⓘ
Robert Smail's Printing Works
EH44 6HA.
Tel: 0844 493 2259
www.nts.org.uk

Me!
(Horace)

By Horace Broon

You would think that with us Broons bein' printed every week in "The Sunday Post" that we would know somethin' about it – printin' I mean. We jist kind of tak it a' for granted, don't we? Did you ever stop and imagine how it's a' done? How ye actually do printin'? We went jist a wee bit further than Peebles tae find oot. Here's ma report . . .

ROBERT SMAIL'S PRINTING WORKS, INNERLEITHEN

The office at Smail's is piled high with invoices, ledgers, old newspapers and all sorts of stuff that they printed over the years. You can see even the records of the passages booked by local folk who emigrated from Scotland with Robert Cowan Smail's shipping agency.

You can see all kinds of examples of printed work from way back in 1877 right up to the present day. The "St. Ronan's Standard and Effective Advertiser" (printed here from 1893 to 1916) made us laugh - advertisements for the best place to buy your "high class artificial teeth" and a "vacuum clothes washer". When it was first published it said it "would not be merely a medium for claptrap and gossip", unlike some papers I can think of.

We had a visit to the Composing Room and learned about a way of printing which lasted over 500 years. The room is filled with rack upon rack of wee pieces of type. Each rack was called a case. The "Upper Case" contained capital letters; the "Lower Case" contained ordinary letters. Computers still use those terms today! We were allowed to pick up the letters and put them in a line on what they call a "stick" and see our names in print - I didn't get it quite right!

Hoarce Broom

The Machine Room contains several printing presses, that go back over a hundred years. The printing machines were powered by a waterwheel until as recently as 1930. Part of the works was built over a river, and they just lowered the waterwheel into the river when they needed some power for the machines.

The printing machines have funny names - the Arab Clamshell Platen, the Wharfedale Reliance, the Original Heidelberg and the Columbian Eagle. They still work today and we were given demonstrations of how they worked.

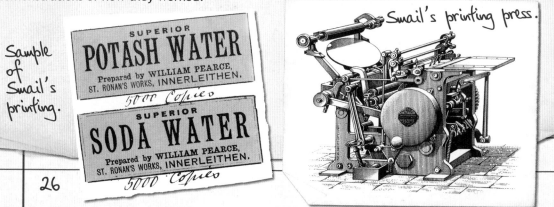

Sample of Smail's printing.

SUPERIOR POTASH WATER
Prepared by WILLIAM PEARCE,
ST. RONAN'S WORKS, INNERLEITHEN.
5000 Copies

SUPERIOR SODA WATER
Prepared by WILLIAM PEARCE,
ST. RONAN'S WORKS, INNERLEITHEN.
5000 Copies

Smail's printing press.

The Borders: places to visit

Abbotsford House

On the banks of the Tweed, Abbotsford was built by Sir Walter Scott, the 19th-century author of classics such as *Waverley*, *Rob Roy* and *Ivanhoe*. It contains an impressive collection of historic relics, weapons and armour (including Rob Roy's gun and Montrose's sword), and a library containing over 9,000 rare volumes.

Country Houses

The Borders contains many grand country houses still lived in by the families that built them. They are open to the public, but check opening times: Floors Castle, Kelso (it's not a castle, but much grander); Manderston House, near Duns; Mellerstain, near Kelso; Paxton House, near Berwick; Thirlestane Castle, near Lauder.

Dryburgh Abbey (near Melrose)

The ruins of this 12th-century abbey are well preserved. The abbey was sacked by English invaders in the 14th and 16th centuries. Sir Walter Scott and Field Marshal Sir Douglas Haig are buried in the abbey.

Flodden Field (in England across the border from Coldstream)

A tall cross in a field marks the site of the 1513 Battle of Flodden when the Scots were routed by the English. King James IV and many Scottish nobles ("the flowers o' the forest") were killed in the battle, along with about 10,000 others, many of whom are buried in St Paul's Church at Branxton, nearby.

Dryburgh Abbey.

Smailholm Tower (near Smailholm)

This small rectangular tower is set within a barmkin wall (a stout defensive wall) on a rocky outcrop and is five storeys high with 7-ft thick walls.

Traquair House (near Peebles)

Dating from the 10th century, this is one of Scotland's oldest inhabited houses. At the end of one of Traquair House's parallel drives is a set of gates that are permanently closed. They were closed behind Bonnie Prince Charlie after he left the house in the autumn of 1745 as the fifth Earl wished him luck and vowed never to open the gates again until a Stuart was on the throne. It also has its own brewery dating from the 18th century. It stopped being used in the early 19th century and its equipment remained untouched until it was rediscovered in 1965, when brewing started again.

Floors Castle.

ⓘ Traquair House EH44 6PW.
Tel: 01896 830323
www.traquair.co.uk

ⓘ Abbotsford House TD6 9BQ.
Tel: 01896 752043
www.scottsabbotsford.co.uk

26 The Sunday Post

Out & About: *The Eildon Hills*

JUST SOUTH of Melrose are the triple peaks of the Eildon Hills. This place is full of history and mystery. There was a fort at the top of North Eildon over 3,000 years ago and the Romans built a very large fort at the bottom of the hills, called Trimontium (three peaks). But then it is said that Thomas the Rhymer met the Fairy Queen here and the hills are the entrance to the Fairy Kingdom, that King Arthur and his Court are asleep under the hill, and that the 13th-century Borders wizard Michael Scott split the original hill into three peaks.

You can walk up the Eildons from Melrose. It will take around 2 hours.

Oor Favourite Museums

Scotland is full of museums — there are hundreds of museums and galleries. There are quite a number mentioned on other pages and I cannae mention all the museums. So I have selected a few more that I like. In addition lots of towns and villages have museums aboot their history — find oot aboot the ones that are close to where you stay.

Aberdeen Maritime Museum

This award-winning museum tells the story of Aberdeen's relationship with the sea, covering ship-building, fishing and the North Sea oil industry. The museum is on Shiprow, overlooking the harbour and incorporating one of Aberdeen's oldest houses, Provost Ross's House, built in 1593. Aberdeen Maritime Museum AB11 5BY. Tel: 01224 337700 www.aagm.co.uk Free

Creetown Gem Rock Museum

This museum displays one of the finest private collections of gemstones, crystals, minerals, rocks and fossils in Great Britain. Gem Rock Museum DG8 7HJ. Tel: 01671 820357 www.gemrock.net Admission charge

Denny Tank, Dumbarton

Discover the world's first commercial ship model experiment tank, the length of a football pitch, and see the ship model mechanism running. Experience the working environment of the model makers, clay moulders and carpenters in 1882. Try your hand at smoothing and carving a real wax hull model. Denny Tank, Dumbarton , G82 1QS. Tel: 01389 763444 www.scottishmaritimemuseum.org/dumbarton. html Admission charge

Dunfermline, Abbot House Heritage Centre

Situated in Dunfermline's historic Maygate, Abbot House, with its pink walls, is one of its most distinctive buildings. With two floors of display rooms, volunteer guides are available to conduct you through 1,000 years of Scottish history.

Abbot House Heritage Centre KY12 7NE. Tel: 01383 733266 www.abbothouse.co.uk Admission charge

Edinburgh, Our Dynamic Earth

Our Dynamic Earth tells the story of Earth from the Big Bang to the present day and even into the future. It explains all aspects of our Earth, from evolution to climate change. Our Dynamic Earth EH8 8AS. Tel: 0131 550 7800 www.dynamicearth.co.uk Admission charge

Fraserburgh, Museum of Scottish Lighthouses

This museum is based around Scotland's first mainland lighthouse, built in 1797 for the Commissioners of Northern Lights and built on top of the 16th-century Kinnaird Castle. The museum tells the story of how lighthouses work and the people that used to look after them. Museum of Scottish Lighthouses AB43 9DU. Tel: 01346 511022 www.lighthousemuseum.org. uk Admission charge

Glasgow, Hunterian Museum

Part of the University of Glasgow this museum, recently modernised, contains an outstanding collection of fossils, archaeological remains, and much on the history of science and medicine. Hunterian Museum G12 8QQ. Tel: 0141 330 4221 www.hunterian.gla.ac.uk Free

Summerlee Heritage Park

A museum that looks at the industrial heritage of Central Scotland, with exhibits of industrial machinery, Scotland's only working electric tramway, and a re-created underground mine and miners' cottages from 1840 to 1960. Summerlee Heritage Park ML5 1QD. Tel: 01236 431261 www.northlan.gov.uk Free

This lighthoose jist aboot as big as oor Hen Tee-hee!

29

Dumfries and Galloway

This bit o' Scotland should be better known cos whether it's weddings or wildlife, Burns or beautiful clothes, there's somethin' for ye — and there's ice cream for the Bairn.

Ice Cream!

The Cream o' Galloway visitor centre has an ice cream parlour, a tearoom and shop, as well as a fabulous adventure playground that includes the indoor 'Smugglers' Warren' with its underground tunnels and climbing towers, miles of nature trails and cycle tracks. What about having a go at creating your own ice cream flavour? Make your own ice cream starting from the basic ingredients of milk, cream and sugar, then add your choice from a range of ingredients. The 'Ready Steady Freeze' activity runs during July and August from Monday to Thursday starting at 4 p.m. You get to eat the ice cream that you make!

Enjoying some ice-cream.

ⓘ

For information about Dumfries and Galloway: www.visitdumfriesandgalloway.co.uk
For information about Burns in Dumfries and Galloway: www.burnshowffclub.org
Cream o' Galloway DG7 2DR.
Tel: 01557 814040
www.creamogalloway.co.uk

Wild country

WITH OVER 200 miles of coastline, rolling hills, moorland, forest, mountains and rivers, there is plenty to choose from. The long coastline of the Solway Firth welcomes over 120,000 wildfowl and waders each winter and places such as Caerlaverock and Mersehead Nature Reserve make it easy to get close to flocks of birds.

Galloway Forest Park is the largest forest park in Britain covering over 300 square miles of forest, moorland and lochs rising towards the mountains. It teems with wildlife - red deer, wild goats and red squirrels. Birds of prey also make the forest their home, with buzzards a common sight, golden eagles more elusive and rare red kites, successfully introduced in 2001. Follow the Red Kite Trail and visit the Feeding Station.

Robert Burns

ROBERT BURNS spent much of his adult life in and around Dumfries, dying here aged just 37. While his most famous works such as "Auld Lang Syne" and "Ae Fond Kiss" were written with a romantic and timeless grace in and around Dumfries, he also wrote some of his most politically scathing work here, frustrated by his work as an exciseman and critical of the establishment of the day. You can visit his farm at Ellisland, his house in Dumfries where he died or his favourite howff, The Globe.

National Museum of Costume

Whether you are interested in exploring the house and learning about the costumes or having a picnic on the lawn, there's plenty to see and do at this splendid country house museum set in beautiful wooded grounds. Shambellie House near New Abbey in Dumfries and Galloway presents a fascinating look at fashion and social etiquette from the 1850s to the 1950s. Wonderful room settings with accessories, furniture and paintings complete a graceful Victorian and Edwardian environment of well-to-do living, from parasols to party dresses, linen to lavender bags and samplers to shoes. Leave time to visit Sweetheart Abbey, which is close by.

Sweetheart Abbey

In 1268, Lord John Balliol died. His grieving widow, Lady Dervorgilla of Galloway, had his heart embalmed and placed in an ivory casket. She carried it with her everywhere. She undertook many charitable acts in his memory. These included the founding of the Cistercian abbey of Dulce Cor (Latin for Sweet Heart) in 1273. When she too died in 1289, she was laid to rest in front of the abbey church's high altar, clutching her husband's heart to her bosom. Sweetheart Abbey's conception as a shrine to human and divine love is deeply appealing. So too is its attractive setting. The graceful ruin nestles between the grey bulk of Criffel and the shimmering waters of the Solway Firth, whilst its blood-red sandstone walls contrast with the lush green grass at their feet. Despite the prolonged wars with England, and the vicissitudes of time, the beautiful abbey church of St Mary the Virgin survives almost entire but the monks' cloister to the south has almost entirely gone.

Kirkcudbright

The pretty harbour town of Kirkcudbright is the most well known haven for artists in the region and has acquired the title of Artist's Town for its historical artistic connections. At the turn of the last century it became the focus of an artist's colony which included E A Hornel, who introduced several of the "Glasgow Boys" to the town and eventually settled there permanently in 1895, with his home and garden, Broughton House is now managed by the National Trust for Scotland. As the reputation of the Kirkcudbright School grew it attracted other artists including the distinguished illustrator Jessie M King.

(i)

National Museum of Costume
DG2 8HQ. Tel: 0131 2474030
www.nms.ac.uk/costume
Sweetheart Abbey DG2 8BU
Tel: 01387 850397
www.historic-scotland.gov.uk
Broughton House, Kirkcudbright
DG6 4JX Tel: 0844 493 2246
www.nts.org.uk

Gretna Green

WHEN A law was passed in England saying that no one under the age of 21 could marry without their parents' consent, a new cross Border trade started, for, until 1940, a legal marriage in Scotland could take place in front of two witnesses with no clergy involved. Gretna Green, being the first place over the Border, quickly became a centre for runaway marriages. The local blacksmith soon dominated the trade – and so marriage "over the anvil" at Gretna became established. It is still a very popular place for weddings and for the number of people who visit the Old Blacksmith's shop there.

A few things you dinnae ken aboot Dumfries and Galloway

Dundrennan Abbey is where Mary Queen of Scots spent her last night in Scotland in May 1568.

Ruthwell Cross from the end of the 7th century is considered to be one of the major monuments of Europe in the Dark Ages.

Sanquhar is home to Britain's oldest Post Office, which was first opened in 1763 and operates to this day.

Whithorn is the cradle of Christianity in Scotland and was first founded in the 5th century by St Ninian.

Ayrshire

Ayrshire is the "Land o' Burns" an' its streams, hills, valleys and villages are touched wi' the magic of a poetry that has made their names famous the world over. Ye can find oot more on Robert Burns on page 36. There's more to Ayrshire, however, than Burns an' here are some suggestions.

Ayrshire, which has a coast lined with sandy beaches and fringed with noted golf links, has played its part in Scottish history. The Battle of Largs in 1263 saw the Scots defeat the Vikings and win back the Hebrides and the Isle of Man. William Wallace started on his road to fame as an outlaw in Ayrshire. Robert the Bruce was born at Turnberry Castle, south of Ayr, and Turnberry was the starting point of Bruce's final triumph – lured from his retreat in Arran by a signal fire, he landed here in 1307 to begin the fight for freedom that ended at Bannockburn in 1314.

Bruce wasn't the only king to touch Ayrshire – Elvis Presley touched down at Prestwick Airport on 3 March 1960, the only place in the UK ever to be visited by 'The King'.

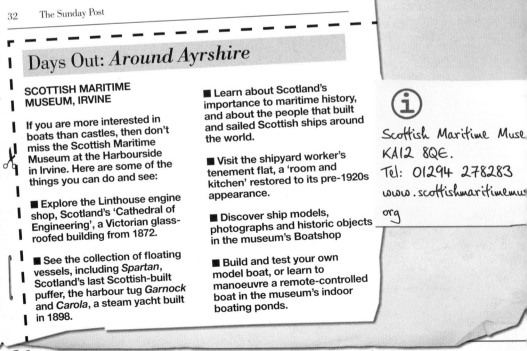

Days Out: *Around Ayrshire*

SCOTTISH MARITIME MUSEUM, IRVINE

If you are more interested in boats than castles, then don't miss the Scottish Maritime Museum at the Harbourside in Irvine. Here are some of the things you can do and see:

■ Explore the Linthouse engine shop, Scotland's 'Cathedral of Engineering', a Victorian glass-roofed building from 1872.

■ See the collection of floating vessels, including *Spartan*, Scotland's last Scottish-built puffer, the harbour tug *Garnock* and *Carola*, a steam yacht built in 1898.

■ Learn about Scotland's importance to maritime history, and about the people that built and sailed Scottish ships around the world.

■ Visit the shipyard worker's tenement flat, a 'room and kitchen' restored to its pre-1920s appearance.

■ Discover ship models, photographs and historic objects in the museum's Boatshop

■ Build and test your own model boat, or learn to manoeuvre a remote-controlled boat in the museum's indoor boating ponds.

ⓘ Scottish Maritime Muse
KA12 8QE.
Tel: 01294 278283
www.scottishmaritimemus
org

Blairquhan, near Maybole, is a fine example of a Regency castle in Scotland, designed by the Scottish architect, William Burn, for Sir David Hunter Blair, 3rd Baronet in 1821-4. It was constructed on the site of a previous castle which dated back to 1346, and has stayed in the possession of the family.

Dunure Castle, located about 5 miles north-west of Maybole, has been a ruin for more than three hundred years. The castle as you see it now is from the 15th and 16th centuries. Here in 1570, Gilbert Kennedy, 4th Earl of Cassillis brought the kidnapped Commendator of Crossraguel Abbey, Alan Stewart, and roasted him over a fire to make him agree to sign away the abbey lands. Stewart was, however, rescued by the Laird of Bargany.

Dunure Castle.

Crossraguel Abbey, near Maybole, is one of a few Cluniac settlements in Scotland, founded in the early 13th century by the Earl of Carrick. The extensive remains of the Abbey are fascinating, and the church, the chapter house and much of the domestic premises can still be viewed.

Culzean – see the next page.

Dean Castle and Country Park is situated on the edge of Kilmarnock. The Castle is a well-preserved 14th-century keep, and the palace block with a tower and curtain wall enclosing a courtyard dates from the 15th century. The castle was restored early in the 20th century. There is a museum with a fine collection of armour and interesting musical instruments. In 1975, the castle and grounds were gifted to the town of Kilmarnock and there is now a country park with a children's area and a farm.

Kelburn Castle, the home of the Earls of Glasgow, is famous for its Castle and historic gardens. It a place of natural beauty with waterfalls, gorges, attractive woodland, dramatic views over the Firth of Clyde and surprises, like the "Secret Forest" adventure area. A great place for a family visit.

(i)

Blairquhan KA19 7LZ.
Tel: 01655 770239
www.blairquhan.co.uk
Crossraguel Abbey KA19 5HQ.
Tel: 01655 883113
www.historic-scotland.gov.uk

The Electric Brae

THE ELECTRIC BRAE, known locally as Croy Brae, is on the A719, south of Dunure, not far from Ayr, and heading towards Maybole. Starting from the bend overlooking Croy railway viaduct, it runs a quarter of a mile to the wooded Craigencroy Glen. Whilst there is a slope of 1 in 86 upwards from the bend at the Glen, the configuration of the land on either side of the road provides an optical illusion making it look as if the slope is going the other way. Therefore, a stationary car on the road with the brakes off will appear to move slowly uphill.

The term "Electric Brae" dates from a time when it was incorrectly thought to be a phenomenon caused by electric or magnetic attraction within the Brae.

(i)

Dean Castle KA3 1XB.
Tel: 01563 522702 FREE
www.deancastle.com
Kelburn Castle KA29 0BE.
Tel: 01475 568685
www.kelburnestate.com

Culzean Castle

Culzean KA19 8LE
Tel: 0844 493 2149
www.nts.org.uk

CULZEAN

CULZEAN IS one of Scotland's best-loved castles and country parks. It has a magnificent cliff-top setting on the South Ayrshire coast off the A719, near Maybole.

Records show there was a tower on the site from the 1400s. By 1759 the Kennedy family transformed the tower into a stately castle and estate – one of the grandest country houses in Scotland.

Robert Adam, the leading Scottish architect of his day, redesigned the house. The elegant circular saloon sits right on top of the cliff with amazing views out to Arran while the oval staircase makes dramatic use of space. The contrast between the ordered house and garden and the wild cliff-edge site make this house very special.

In November 1945 the 5th Marquess and the Kennedy family invited General D Eisenhower, Supreme Commander of the Allied Forces in Europe, to accept the tenancy of a specially created guest flat on the top floor of the Castle for his lifetime, as a gesture of Scottish thanks for American support during the Second World War. He and members of his family stayed at Culzean on several occasions and he also lent it to friends. An exhibition on the first floor of the Castle highlights the achievements of General Eisenhower.

The extensive grounds have a lake, with lilies and ducks and a café that sells ice cream. In clear weather there are stunning views from the battlements to Arran and Ayr and to Ailsa Craig, that enormous lump of rock a few miles out to sea. There is a vine, rose garden and rhododendrons and lots of countryside to explore, as well as a wonderful beach surrounded by rocks, where you can swim. Down by the sea is the old Gas House, where gas was made for use in the house, and in the rocky cliffs are caves once used by pirates. There's a Visitor Centre in the old Stables, to tell you all about what is going on at Culzean. As one of Scotland's most visited places, there's always something happening!

35

A Day Oot wi Burns

"TO A HOOSE"
by Horace BRUNE

My perfect day oot,
Withoot a doot,
Is ambling doon
Tae Alloway Toon.

To a very SPECIAL hoose, actually. I love poetry and have read almost everything written by Mr Robert Burns, OOR RABBIE.

A cottage in the wee village of Alloway in Ayrshire is the birthplace of Scotland's favourite son. I have "the muse" within me and have fantasies that Robert Burns, whose father's name was BURNES, was actually born Robert BRUNES, which is the old spelling of BROONS, and that I am Rabbie's great-great-great-(very good)-grandson poet.

BURNS NATIONAL HERITAGE PARK in Alloway is of course my favourite place in Scotland. In one day, you can visit on foot the cottage where Burns was born and the museum next to it, stroll through the village, take in the Tam o' Shanter Experience exhibit, visit the Burns Monument, the Brig o' Doon . . . and sit in the graveyard of the Auld Kirk of Alloway, where Tam o' Shanter on his mare Meg first glimpsed Cutty Sark and the witches and warlocks dancing in a bleeze. And if you are brave, after the day out is done, visit the graveyard at night and shut your eyes and IMAGINE. WOOO . . .! Scary. Better you than me.

BURNS COTTAGE is where Rabbie was born on 25th January 1759. Built by Rabbie's father William Burnes, the cottage is in its original condition. There's an audio-visual display that brings to life what it was like in those days. I got goosebumps being in the very room where Rabbie came into the world as the January winds blasted outside the family's new cottage. Epic!

BURNS COTTAGE MUSEUM has the original manuscript of "Auld Lang Syne", Granpaw's favourite song. It's probably better known than any other song in the English language.

TAM O' SHANTER EXPERIENCE is a theatre where technology brings this most fantastic poem to life. Follow Tam on his way home from the pub on his horse Meg. Watch as the tipsy eejit comes to Alloway Auld Kirk graveyard and roars out to Cutty Sark and get gripped as the witches and warlocks chase Tam over the Brig o' Doon and snatch off poor Meg's tail. Ouch!

Then you can climb up the Burns Monument and get a rare view of the village where Rabbie grew up. You can see the ruins of Alloway Auld Kirk and its eerie graveyard. Stand at the keystone of the Brig o' Doon where the ghouls and ghosts couldn't cross the water and feel Tam's relief and Meg's sore bottom as the pair escaped.

Now, as days oot go, this one is just sheer poetry!

36

Kirkoswald Churchyard

In this churchyard are the graves of Burns' schoolmaster Hugh Rodger, of John Davidson (Souter Johnnie) and Douglas Graham (Tam o' Shanter).

A SCOTTISH TOURIST BOARD PROJECT

Auld Brig o' Doon, Alloway.

ROBERT BURNS

Burns cottage.

ⓘ Burns National Heritage Park
KA7 4PQ. Tel: 01292 443700
www.burnsheritagepark.com
More info: Robert Burns
Birthplace Museum project
www.nts.org.uk/burns

37

On Arran

Daphne

MY FAVOURITE DAY OOT
by Daphne Broon

Maw asked wid I write tae Uncle Doogie in Australia an' tell him aboot ma favourite day oot. She really wants Doogie tae come an' visit us, so we'll wait an' see. This is my idea o' a perfect day - me an' Maggie went wi' Joe and Hen on hire bikes while we were holidayin' on Arran wi' the gang.

I fair enjoyed the boat "crossin' fae Ardrossan" (that's a rhyme by the way!). Caledonian MacBrayne boats are the biz and the breakfasts are tae die for. Try the full Scottish fry-up! The boat lands at Brodick and ye can walk tae <u>BRODICK CASTLE</u> and Gardens fae the boat, or get the bus if ye must. The bairns wanted tae hire bikes as weel, but Arran's a richt hilly place. Jist HOW hilly Hen didna mention until later.

We cycled fae Brodick tae the north o' the island past a wee place ca'd Corrie wi' a bonnie harbour facing across the Clyde. I should hae stopped there!! Three miles up the road the hill fae Sannox tae Lochranza wiz like biking over Ben Nevis wi' lumps on it. I pushed the bike a' the way UP the hill. Efter catchin' ma breath at the summit for aboot half an 'oor and twa sandwiches, the freewheel tae Lochranza was better than the Blackpool Pleasure Beach. Afore I kent where I was, I was sittin' in the <u>LOCHRANZA DISTILLERY VISITOR CENTRE.</u> Dinna miss it. The range o' malts is fantastic. I bocht a miniature and rubbed it intae ma thighs tae stop the pain . . . and their scones and jam are pain free. I had six.

(i) Lochranza Distillery
Visitor Centre KA27 8HJ.
Tel: 01770 830264
www.arranwhisky.com

(i) Caledonian MacBrayne:
Ardrossan KA22 8ED.
Tel: 01294 463470
Brodick KA27 8AY.
Tel: 01770 302166
www.calmac.co.uk

Brodick Castle gardens - beautiful.

Lochranza.

Back on the bike, it was doon the west coast, wi' lovely views oot tae the Kintyre Peninsula. This no-sae-wee stretch o' road is as bonnie a spot as ye'll find. At <u>MACHRIE</u>, where ye can visit the <u>STANDIN' STANES</u> (me, I could hardly stand masel' by this time), we turned east through the middle o' the island back towards Brodick.

Ye can cycle farther doon an' dae the hale circuit if ye're like Lance Armstrong or Hen Broon, but it's too far for the fuller figure (nae laughin'!). And of course, nae prizes for guessin' there's ANITHER muckle hill tae cycle. It's ca'd the String Road, but I remember it as the STING Road. I dinna ken whether it was the whisky wearin' aff or the muscle strain, but ma legs were on fire. But I made it tae the tap withoot gettin' aff . . . Hen gied me a tow!

Doon the brae again like the wind and it was intae the <u>ARRAN CHEESE SHOP</u> and the <u>ARRAN BREWERY</u>, jist near the Castle where we'd started.

Standin' stanes at Machrie

ⓘ

Isle of Arran Brewery Visitor Centre KA27 8DE.
Tel: 01770 302353
www.arranbrewery.com
Island Cheese Company KA27 8DD.
Tel: 01770 302788
www.islandcheese.co.uk

Now, back wi' the family at the Castle, we had a rare visit. The main rooms are on the first floor, so ye hae tae help aulder folk up the stairs. Granpaw was a star . . . he helped me a' the way up. Ma legs were like jelly fae the bikin'. The gardens are richt bonnie and we had a picnic on the grass wi' Maw's corned beef sandwiches, Dundee Cake and a flask o' coffee (wi' a wee smidgeon suggestion o' ten-year-auld Lochranza!). There are heiland coos, woodland trails and the waterfalls. Ane o' the laddies fell in the burn, but that's normal on a Broons' day oot.

I was mair than pleased wi' MY day and although I was tired I'd dae it a' again ony day . . .on the back o' Sandy Bell's motorbike!! Hen wanted us a' tae go up Goatfell the next day but THIS auld goat was fell knackered and I spent the next day wi' Maggie at the AUCHRANNIE SPA RESORT. BLLLLLISS!

Cask Matured APPLE & ARRAN ALE

Chutney

ISLE OF ARRAN BREWERY

Net Wt. 6.3oz 180g ℮

Brodick Castle.

ISLE OF ARRAN DISTILLERY

Isle of ARRAN Cheese Shop

(i)
Brodick Castle, Garden & Country Pa
KA27 8HY. Tel: 0844 493 2152
Country Park Ranger
Tel: 0844 493 2155
www.nts.org.uk
Auchrannie Spa Resort KA27 8BZ Te
01770 302234
www.auchrannie.co.uk

Inside Lochranza distillery.

Brodick Castle

Brodick Castle sits on sheltered land overlooking Brodick Bay. The Vikings used the site first, but the oldest parts of the castle now dates from the 13th century. James IV granted the castle to his cousin, James Hamilton, in 1503, and made him Earl of Arran at the same time. The East Tower was built in 1588 and extended when the castle was occupied by Cromwell's troops in the 1650s. The 10th Duke of Hamilton greatly extended the castle in the 1840s and remodelled much of the inside in what was then a fashionable Jacobean style. The castle contains a precious collection of oil paintings and antique furniture once owned by the Dukes of Hamilton. The wonderful gardens were created in the last century and contain an internationally renowned collection of over 200 different rhododendron species. Beyond the gardens is the Brodick Country Park, with many woodland trails and an abundance of wildlife.

Goatfell

Towering above the castle are Arran's rocky mountains, the highest being Goatfell at 2,866 ft (874 metres). To climb it you need good boots and you need to stick to the paths unless you are an experienced mountaineer. From the summit you can see Ben Lomond, the island of Jura and across the Clyde to Ayr and even the coast of Ireland on a good day. The start of the walk up Goatfell starts opposite the Brodick Country Park.

PRODUCT

Es

Arran
M

SINGLE
MALT
SCOTCH
WHISKY

DISTILLED, MATURED AND BOTTLED
IN SCOTLAND,
ISLE OF ARRAN DISTILLERS LTD, ARRAN.

0cl ℮ 46%Alc./Vol 46% V

AGED **12** YEARS

Lochranza distillery.

The Waverley

Joe

DOON THE WATTER
by Joe Broon

"Doon the Watter". It's an expression near a'body in Glasgow knows only too well. For a'body else, it's takin' a boat doon the Clyde to the Firth o' Clyde and the islands beyond.

And now it's "Doon the Watter" on the loveliest ship in the world. Nane o' yer ocean-goin' cruise liners can haud a candle tae the <u>WAVERLEY</u>. It's the last sea-going paddle steamer in the world. But dinna run awa' wi' the idea that this is some battered auld relic o' a bygone age. Launched on the Clyde in 1947, Waverley was bought by a bunch of enthusiasts from CalMac in 1974 for <u>ONE POUND</u>. Bargain or what!! Restored in the year 2000, The Waverley is majestic. Some folk jist turn up at the pier tae see her. Red and white towering funnels, polished timber and gleaming brass, this ship is the pride o' the Clyde. Folk come fae all over tae sail doon the watter tae here, there and everywhere. And ye canna sing "I Belong tae Glasgow" if ye havenae been doon the Clyde on the boat.

I like tae turn up at the pier at <u>GLASGOW LANCEFIELD QUAY</u> wi' my accordion under ma arm and play us a' oot doon the watter. A few foot-tappin' tunes soon gets a'body in the mood. But if accordion music's no' yer taste and ye canna shak' a leg at "Strip the Willow", ye can jist stand on deck and hear the music o' the mighty twin paddles swooshing the waters o' the Clyde ahent us, and breathe in the air. Or, if ye like mighty orchestra music, head doon intae the bowels o' the ship and visit the engine room. It's deafening doon there, wi' the enormous pistons o' the steam engine hammering oot the chorus of the ship's ain Clyde music. And the smell o' the hot grease will soon clear ony sair heids fae the night before.

And it's no' jist the near-at-hand ports ye can visit like Greenock and Dunoon and Largs and Rothesay and so on. The Waverley will tak' you an' yer sea legs tae amongst other spots, Armadale on Skye, Tobermory, Fort William, Brodick, Campbeltown and Ayr. And my favourite destination is Inverie on Knoydart. Ye'll get a rare welcome fae the accordion lovers at the Old Forge pub there!!

Overlooking Gourock and the Clyde from the Free French Memorial at Greenock.

ⓘ

Waverley Excursions G3 8HA
Tel 0141 221 8152
www. waverleyexcursions.co.u
Waverley enthusiasts
www.pswaverley.org

A Day Out On The Waverley

THE WAVERLEY only sails at certain times between Easter and October. It travels off to other parts of the country during its season. You will need to check on its sailing times. This is best done online at the Waverley Excursions website (www.waverleyexcursions.co.uk) or by telephone (0141 221 8152) or at the Glasgow terminal (Waverley Terminal, 36 Lancefield Quay, Glasgow G3 8HA).

Weekend sailings can be very busy, so it's wise to book. If your holiday dates don't match the Waverley's sailings, you might be able to get aboard Waverley's sister ship the motor vessel the BALMORAL. It's not a paddle steamer but it is a historic pleasure cruiser.

But get online or phone. This is one time you really don't want to MISS THE BOAT. Come on doon!! . . . Doon the Watter!

The pier at Rothesay.

PIER CLOCK, DUNOON

THE WAVERLEY APPROACHES DUNOON

GREETINGS FROM DUNOON

HOLY LOCH

JB210961

The Waverley.

New Lanark

THE MILLS ARE ALIVE WITH THE SOUND OF MUSIC
by Maggie Broon

I'd aye read stories in "The Bunty" and the like when I was young aboot orphans and cruel mill owners, stories that kept me aff my sleep. In Scotland, there's a village less than an hour fae Glasgow and Edinburgh that was once a monument to the "good" mill owners. It's now a World Heritage Site and it's called NEW LANARK, a beautifully restored living village in a bonnie setting on a bend in the River Clyde. It's richt below the Falls of Clyde. The Clyde's waters powered the cotton mills that David Dale built over 200 years ago. Dale's son-in-law Robert Owen provided decent hooses for the workers, fair wages, FREE health care and a new education system for his employees, includin' the first nursery school in the world. He tellt his workers in 1816 that society could exist withoot crime, withoot poverty, with good health service, little misery and wi' intelligence and happiness increased. Some guy he must hae been.

It was jist me an' Daphne that visited New Lanark, but we'll tak' a' the family with us next time we go. Ye can easily spend a happy day here.

At the Visitor Centre there's a thing ca'd "The Annie McLeod Experience Ride". It takes ye intae the spirit world of New Lanark and ye travel back in time. It's awfy excitin'. We were taken on a fascinatin' journey o' discovery by the ghost of mill girl Annie McLeod who magically appears and tells her ain story of life in New Lanark in 1820. Ye can wander around the village and it's easy to imagine how people lived and worked in Owen's time, and you can explore all the attractions in the Visitor Centre with just one passport ticket.

Ye can also see in the restored houses how the village workers lived and ye can pop in tae Robert Owen's ain hoose. No' many mill owners wid let ye dae that nowadays. We took hame some wool yarn spun on the restored 19th century mill machinery. I canna tell a lie, though. We took hame some NEW stuff fae the shops in the Mill No. 2, braw knitwear and cashmere.

We finished aff oor day wi' a lovely walk fae the FALLS OF CLYDE VISITOR CENTRE (run by the Scottish Wildlife Trust) through the woods tae the big waterfall at Corra Linn. Fascinatin' tae think this is the same watter that runs doon under the Kingston Bridge and floated a' thae big ships that Glasgow once made.

Ye can get tae New Lanark by bus or train tae Lanark itself and there's a link bus every hour fae the Lanark Tourist Info Centre. Only aboot a mile. It's a lovely day oot and it really is a wee gem.

New Lanark.

Preston Mill EH40 3DS.
Tel: 0844 493 2128.
www.nts.org.uk

Stanley Mills PH1 4QE.
Tel 01738 828268
www.historic-scotland.gov.uk

New Lanark
WORLD HERITAGE SITE

Expect the unexpected!

Explore one of Scotland's top visitor attractions,
less than an hour from Edinburgh & Glasgow

UNESCO
WORLD
HERITAGE
SITE

European
Heritage
Medal
Winner

British
Tourism
Trophy

Scottish
Tourism
Oscar

Heritage

New Lanark ML11 9DB.
Tel: 01555 661345
www.newlanark.org

Falls of Clyde Visitor Centre
ML11 9DB. Tel: 01555 665262
www.swt.org.uk

A day out to the mills

Preston Mill

In East Lothian, near East Linton, visit PRESTON MILL. Powered by water this mill grinds oats to get as much as possible from the grains, including flour and oatmeal (it is often referred to as a meal mill). Stunningly picturesque, the present buildings date from the 18th century, though there has been a mill on this site since the 16th century. The mill was used commercially until 1959 and visitors can still experience the working machinery on a tour today. There is an exhibition room to tell you about the mill, those that lived there, and the life of a miller. Close by is the Phantassie Doocot. It is about 500 years old. When it was built, the birds that were kept in the doocot were used for food.

North of Perth is another cotton mill, STANLEY MILLS, on the banks of the Tay. Stanley Mills is one the best-preserved relics of the 18th-century Industrial Revolution. It was established as a cotton mill by local merchants, with support from the English cotton baron Richard Arkwright. Textiles were produced here for 200 years. The mills, and Stanley village built for the workers, were built from the 1780s onwards at a bend in the river, where tremendous water-power was available. It is now possible to explore the mill buildings and discover the many changes that took place over two centuries. The Visitor Centre tells the stories of those who worked there and the products they made. The interactive displays let you discover if your fingers are as nimble as a child labourer's or compete to see if you are tough enough in business to make the mills profitable. Hear the clamour of the factory floor and see how engineers harnessed the energy of the Tay as well as the machinery that turned raw cotton into products sold around the world.

A Day of Rural Life

Nae a trip tae the But an' Ben, but a visit tae the National Museum o' Rural Life on the edge o' East Kilbride. While there aboots, visit Blantyre tae see the birthplace o' David Livingstone, oor great African explorer an' missionary, but check for information afore visitin' as there are changes bein' made in 2009.

The National Museum of Rural Life

THE EDGE of the new town of East Kilbride might seem an unlikely place to find a museum of rural life – but it does mean it is easy for lots of people to get to it. It's a fairly new museum (the main building was only finished in 2001) and consists of two parts, a museum building which contains lots of exhibits about farming, which has been created from the collection of the National Museum of Scotland and, close by, a 170-acre working 1950s farm, Wester Kittochside, that belongs to the National Trust for Scotland. Linking the two, you can enjoy the tractor ride provided between the two sites.

The Museum

The Museum building has three main galleries covering the land, the people who worked the land and the tools they used. Together they tell the story of Scottish country life from around 1750 onwards. You can learn about how we changed the landscape to meet our needs, how people were affected by poor harvests and how tools helped to increase food production and change the landscape.

You can follow the progress of farm machinery from horse-pulled equipment through to the combine harvester and see the Clayton Combine, the first European-built combine harvester. There are also lots of tractors to see, including a cut-away tractor that you can see working when you press the button! Find out about how Scotland led the way with many farming innovations across two centuries of rapid change.

The Farm

The Wester Kittochside farm has never been intensively cultivated so that the Reid family, who farmed the land for generations, gifted the museum an environmentally rich and diverse farm, with many traditional rural features that have vanished elsewhere. The farm illustrates the period of intense change around 1950, which allows visitors to look back to man- and horse-power and forward to the tractor and combine harvester.

Following the pattern of seasonal work, you can see ploughing, seed time, haymaking and harvest. You can also see cows being milked and sheep and chickens being reared using traditional methods. The farm house and the steadings around the house, including the stables and the milking parlour, are also open. Depending on the time of year, there will be different things to see on the farm and there is a big programme of activities throughout the year.

(i)

National Museum of Rural Life G76 9HR. Tel: 0131 247 4369 www.nms.ac.uk/rural

David Livingstone Centre G72 9BY. Tel: 0844 493 2207 www.nts.org.uk Check before visiting.

47

Glasgow: Kelvingrove Museum

"LET US HASTE TO KELVINGROVE, BONNIE LASSIE O . . ."
by Paw Broon

As a day oot in Glasgow, a visit tae <u>KELVINGROVE MUSEUM</u> has tae be number one on anybody's list. BUT, ye'd be surprised tae learn how many folk fae Glasgow have never been through its doors . . . and that's a shame, so get aff yer backside, get there and see what ye've been missing.

Get aff the wee orange underground train (some folk ca' it the Subway) at Kelvinhall and it's a ten minute stroll tae the venue or get aff at Hillhead and hae a family stroll doon lively Byres Road or even doon fae Kelvinbridge and through <u>KELVINGROVE PARK</u>. That's really bonnie.

My lot get aff at Kelvinhall and tak' a wee diversion up Byres Road to the legendary University Cafe. Hasnae changed in years. This wee gem was founded by an Italian fae Barga in Tuscany. Seems half Barga's population emigrated years ago tae Scotland tae open chip shops, ice cream parlours and the like. And I'm glad they did!

Early coffees and munchies snaffled, head for Kelvingrove Museum. It really is a fantastic sight. World famous and rightly so. Glasgow is and should be rightly sae proud o' this . . . and it's FREE tae get in. Handy when yer family numbers eleven. The building originally cost £250,000 tae build and as ye'll probably know that might buy ye a guid tenement flat in Partick now if ye're lucky. Recently completely renovated at the cost o' nearly £30 million it's been worth every penny.

Kelvingrove is probably Glasgow's favourite building and ye can easily see why. Its big towers I'm tellt were inspired by the great pilgrimage kirk of Santiago de Compostela in Spain. And it's nae exaggeration tae say that the building itself is as worthy o' interest as the stuff inside. And what stuff. There's something here for everybody and that's everybody of a' ages. It wid be impossible for the likes o' me tae describe what's here.

Get ane' o' the leaflets or guide books at the shops inside and just wander aboot gawpin'. It's that good. As I read in ane o' the guides, "one of the finest collections in Europe". Oor family jist loved it, and we've been back dozens o' times. Granpaw and me even managed tae sneak oot for a "hauf an' a hauf" an' naebody missed us. If ye're five or ninety-five, haste ye tae Kelvingrove!

Kelvingrove Park.

Charles Rennie Mackintosh designed furniture.

(i)

Kelvingrove Art Gallery and Museum G3 8AG.
FREE
Tel: 0141 276 9599
www.glasgowmuseums.com

Nae Park-in'... get it? Tee hee!

Statue

of Lord

Kelvin.

14   The Scots Magazine

Kelvingrove is No. 1 in Scotland!

The Kelvingrove Art Gallery and Museum was the top attraction in Scotland according to the 2008 survey by the Association of Leading Visitor Attractions, with 1,445,098 people visiting during the year - and it was the 13th most popular attraction throughout the UK. The first 12 are all in London. The second most popular attraction in Scotland was Edinburgh Castle.

Part of the Charles Rennie Mackintosh tearoom display.

Just the richt location for an auld relic like Granpaw!

49

Glasgow: The Tenement House

Tenement House G3 6QN.
Tel: 0844 493 2197
www.nts.org.uk

THE TENEMENT HOUSE
by Maw Broon

Now, wha would hae believed it? Me visitin' a museum that's really jist anither tenement hoose like oors and lovin' every minute o' it. An' me that's been naggin' awa' at Paw for fifty years an' mair tae move us tae a nice bungalow wi' a wee gairden.

This particular tenement flat is in Glasgow at No. 145 Buccleuch Street in Garnethill. It's only a five-minute walk fae Sauchiehall Street near where the M8 roars by.

The TENEMENT HOUSE was built in 1892 and it still looks today exactly like it did when it was built. A lot o' that's due tae the fact it was owned by the same woman for 50 years. Inside the hoosie, it's like steppin' back in time tae when Glasgow was the industrial power hoose o' the British Empire. There's the auld-fashioned bed recesses and lots o' period furniture. It looks like a film set fae a Victorian television series. There was even a lovely auld Grandfather Clock. The kitchen range was great tae see. It's original and once upon a time we a' had them. It brought back sae many happy memories. Mind you, I still prefer ma new gas cooker.

The building itself is spotless tae. A puckle o' Glasgow tenements I ken could well dae wi' haein' a look at how things SHOULD look. But although the hoose itsel' hasna changed in near ower a hunner an' twenty years, the outlook fae the flat certainly has. I shudder tae think how many cars and trucks race past on the M8 that ye can see jist ootside the front window.

This is a wee gem and well worth visitin'. I've been back a few times and had a rare time. Now I'm off doon the road for a wee Chicken Rogan Josh. Nane o' that in 1892 I'll bet!

I think Horace has spilled curry on his typin. Hee Hee

THE TENEMENT HOUSE
145 Buccleuch Street, Garnethill (third left off Rose St or Cambridge St, NW of Sauchiehall Street pedestrian shopping area), Glasgow city centre. G3 6QN

A typical Victorian tenement flat of 1892, this was the home of a shorthand typist for over 50 years, and little has changed since the early 20th century. It retains many original fittings, including the splendid kitchen range, and fascinating family items. Exhibition on tenement life.
• Shop
1 Mar to 31 Oct, daily 1–5.

WEAVER'S COTTAGE

More tae do in Glasgow

The Scots Magazine

There are tons o' things tae do in Glasgow. Here are a few of oor favourites (and guess who likes the shops . . ?)

Glasgow Cathedral

The Cathedral is the largest surviving medieval building in Scotland and is dedicated to Glasgow's patron saint, St Mungo. It was mainly built in the 13th century and provides a remarkable reminder of what Glasgow might have been like before the Industrial Revolution. It's well worth a visit and it is free to go in. While there, you could visit the Necropolis, a grand cemetery for the good and the great of the city, which is next to the Cathedral, and also the St Mungo Museum of Religious Life and Art and Glasgow's one medieval house, Provand's Lordship.

Glasgow Cathedral G4 0QZ. FREE
Tel: 0141 552 8198 www.glasgowcathedral.org.uk
For the St Mungo Museum and Provand's Lordship, visit:
www.glasgowmuseums.com

The Museum of Transport

The Museum of Transport is across the road from the Kelvingrove Museum (until it moves into a new building by the Clyde in 2011). It has old cars and trams and trains (and a re-creation of an old Glasgow Street) as well as an amazing collection of detailed models of ships made on the Clyde. As with all Glasgow museums, entrance is free.

Museum of Transport G3 8DP. FREE
Tel: 0141 287 2720 www.glasgowmuseums.com

The Glasgow Science Centre

For all who want a hands-on experience of science this is the place to go. As well as the interactive exhibits, there is a planetarium and an IMAX cinema. There is also a 300-ft tower (with a lift) – from the top you will see great views of the city, but check first to see if it's open as it sometimes has to shut for maintenance and because it's too windy.

Glasgow Science Centre G51 1EA.
Tel: 0871 540 1000 www. glasgowsciencecentre.org
Admission charge.

The People's Palace

The People's Palace is Glasgow's social history museum and tells the story of the people and city of Glasgow from 1750 to the present. After seeing the museum, you can relax in the Winter Gardens, a vast Victorian conservatory attached to the museum.

People's Palace G40 1AT. FREE
Tel: 0141 276 0788 www.glasgowmuseums.com

The Burrell Collection

Sir William Burrell was an inveterate collector. He left his enormous collection of over 9,000 pictures, sculptures, tapestries, ceramics and artefacts from ancient Egypt to the French impressionists to the city of Glasgow. The collection is housed in a dramatic building built 25 years ago in Pollok Country Park and provides an exhilarating introduction to the arts of the world. Close by is Pollok House, an 18th-century country house (admission charge). The country park has lots of walks and its own herd of Highland cows.

The Burrell Collection G43 1AT. FREE
Tel: 0141 287 2550 www.glasgowmuseums.com

The Shops

And of course, there are the shops, what with Glasgow being one of the best shopping cities of Europe. There will be something to tempt anyone among all the choice available, from the jewellers in the Argyll Arcade to the big shops in the Buchanan Galleries. Buchanan Street is the heart of the shopping area. Visit Princes Square and then walk through to the specialist shops in the Merchant City.

Botanic Gardens

Botanic Gardens

Glasgow's Botanic Gardens are located at Kelvinside in Glasgow's West End between the River Kelvin, Great Western Road and Queen Margaret Drive.

The Kibble Palace Glasshouse, situated within the Botanic Gardens, is one of the most amazing iron and glass buildings remaining from the Victorian era. The main part of the building formed a conservatory at John Kibble's home at Coulport on Loch Long. He dismantled it in 1872 and it was taken up the Clyde by barge and by cart to the Botanic Gardens, where it was re-assembled and enlarged. Restored in a multi-million pound project completed in November 2006, it has a national collection of tree ferns in and amongst which are a selection of Victorian marble sculptures, including "Eve" by Scipione Tadolini.

In the main range of glasshouses there are several important collections including tropical orchids and begonias, and in the park, as well as sweeping expanses of grass, there are many special trees and shrubs. There is a 200-year-old weeping ash tree, and large black oaks and beech trees. Other key features of Glasgow's Botanics are the world rose garden, a herb garden, an uncommon vegetable garden and a flower garden.

Scotland's Botanic Gardens are ace. Scotland loves its gardens.

(i)

Glasgow's Botanic Gardens
G12 0UE. FREE
Tel: 0141 276 1614
www.glasgow.gov.uk and
search for "Botanic Gardens"

Edinburgh's Botanic Gardens at Inverleith comprise 70 acres of stunning scenery, just a stone's throw from the city centre. Home to the largest collection of wild-origin Chinese plants outside China, including many rhododendrons, the Botanics are also worth visiting for their collection of heathers, the world-famous rock garden, and the 400 ft-long herbaceous border, which is backed by a 100-year-old beech hedge as well as its conifers and Sierra redwoods from North America. There is a also a special tour of climatic zones. There is a charge to enter the glasshouses.

The garden was first established in 1670 near Holyrood Abbey, for the "culture and importation of foreign plants", and was one of Britain's first botanic gardens. It moved to the head of Nor' Loch, now the site of Waverley Station and then in 1763 to a site on the road to Leith. In 1820 it moved again to Inverleith, but this move took three years, and used transplanting machines invented by the curator, William McNab, for the mature trees.

During the last century Edinburgh's Botanics acquired three regional gardens – Benmore, in Argyll, Dawyck, in the wooded hills of the Scottish Borders and Logan in Dumfries and Galloway.

Dundee Botanic Garden is open throughout the year, and is situated near Dundee's airport. Dundee prides itself on running a low-cost garden that was established on a shoestring in 1966. The founding principles of the garden are science, education and conservation. A Visitor's Centre was opened in 1984. A feature of the garden is the "native plant communities unit" that contains a representative range of plants that grow within the British Isles. Trees are now also a major part of the display, and include birch, ash, oak, beech and pine. Exotic plants include a Brazilian fern and plants that have adapted to different environments.

Duthie Park, Aberdeen, by the banks of the River Dee, is a park of 44 acres which was donated to the city by Lady Elizabeth Duthie in 1880 and opened to the public in 1883. Within the park is the spectacular David Welch Winter Gardens, which were rebuilt in 1970 after the original glasshouses of 1899 were badly damaged in a storm. These house many exotic plants including tree ferns, Spanish moss, banana trees and one of the largest collections of cacti in Britain. The park has many other features including a Japanese Garden, a bandstand, fountains, ponds and statues. This is a park for all the family, with activities from boating in the ponds to cricket on the lawns.

ⓘ
Royal Botanic Gardens
EH3 5LR. FREE
Tel: 0131 552 7171
www.rbge.org.uk

Florist delightus, Tee-hee!

ⓘ
University of Dundee Botanic
Garden DD2 1QH.
Tel: 01382 381190
www.dundeebotanicgarden.co.uk

ⓘ
Duthie Park and Winter Garden
AB11 7TH. Tel: 01224 583155
www.aberdeencity.gov.uk FREE

53

Glasgow: Charles Rennie Mackintosh

Glasgow has a world-famous architect and he was called
Charles Rennie Mackintosh. Here's what I've found oot aboot him.

CHARLES RENNIE MACKINTOSH

Charles Rennie Mackintosh is recognised internationally as "the father of the Glasgow style" and as a major influence in the development of modern architecture – and all his most famous buildings are in Glasgow or close by.

He was born in 1868 and lived in Dennistoun. Aged fifteen, he began evening classes at Glasgow School of Art. Towards the end of the 19th century, the art school was one of the leading art academies of Europe. A year later Mackintosh joined John Hutchison's architectural practice as an apprentice draughtsman. In 1889 he joined the larger architectural practice of Honeyman and Keppie, where he later became a partner in 1901. In 1900 Mackintosh married Margaret Macdonald, whom he met at Glasgow School of Art. She was key influence on his interior designs. Over the next few years he designed the buildings he is famous for. They left Glasgow in 1913, and Mackintosh spent most of the rest of his life in the south of France, where he painted. Both he and his wife died in London. Today Mackintosh is celebrated for his skill and talent as an architect, designer and watercolourist.

The most significant buildings that he designed in Glasgow include the Glasgow School of Art, Glasgow Herald offices (now the Lighthouse architecture and design museum), the Willow Tearooms, Scotland Street School, Queen's Cross Church, The Hill House in Helensburgh and Windyhill in Kilmacolm.

THE GLASGOW SCHOOL OF ART tOUR→

Charles Rennie Mackintosh's greatest architectural achievement.

The best Mackintosh buildings.

The Hill House, Helensburgh

The Hill House is rated as Mackintosh's finest house. With views over the Clyde at Helensburgh, and designed for the publisher Walter Blackie in 1902, the house's design, furniture and formal gardens are classic Mackintosh style. It is now run by the National Trust for Scotland and is open from April to October. The Hill House G84 9AJ. Tel: 0844 493 2208 www.nts.org.uk   Admission charge

Scotland Street School

Designed in 1903-6, Scotland Street School has been restored to Mackintosh's original designs. It was the last major building by Mackintosh in Glasgow. The building is now a museum of education and contains three classroom reconstructions to show the changing nature of the schoolroom from the Victorian era, through the Second World War to the classroom of the 1950s. There are interactive displays and exhibitions.

Scotland Street School G5 8QB. Tel: 0141 287 0500 www.glasgowmuseums.com   FREE

Glasgow School of Art

Mackintosh's design for the new Glasgow School of Art in 1896 was the birth of a new style in 20th-century European architecture. Since the extension that he designed in 1906, which includes his spectacular library, the building has remained the heart of the art school. Regular tours are run for visitors to the building.

Glasgow School of Art G3 6RQ. Tel: 0141 353 4500 www.gsa.ac.uk   Admission charge

The Willow Tea Rooms

Mackintosh was commissioned by Kate Cranston to create all four of her Glasgow tea rooms. During a 20-year partnership, he designed wall murals, furniture and all other aspects of the tea rooms. Tea, and the social act of drinking it, was very important then, and in 1903 the Willow Tea Rooms in Sauchiehall Street extended over four floors. The Room de Luxe had silver-painted furniture and leaded mirror friezes, while those Ingram Street had a Chinese Room, with lattice-style screens. The rooms have been re-created today to give an idea of their former glory.

Willow Tea Rooms, Sauchiehall Street G2 3EX 0141. Tel: 0141 332 0521, and Buchanan Street G1 3HF. Tel: 0141 204 5242   www.willowtearooms.co.uk

The Hill Hoose.

Queens Cross Church

The only church designed by Mackintosh, it has recently been restored and is the home of the Charles Rennie Mackintosh Society.

Queens Cross Church G20 7EL. Tel: 0141 946 6600   www.crmsociety.com Admission charge

Hunterian Art Gallery

Mackintosh's own house has been reconstructed here and furnished with many examples of Mackintosh furniture from the University of Glasgow's collection.

Hunterian Art Gallery G12 8QQ. Tel: 0141 330 5431   www.hunterian.gla.ac.uk Admission charge to Mackintosh House

Oor Favourite Art Galleries

ABOOT ART GALLERIES

I dinnae think we had ever all been in a Gallery together till we were caught in the rain an' took shelter - but what a magical world we found inside. There's paintings from hunners of years ago that look as if the paint's no dry yet. There are portraits of how folk used to look and how they dressed (or didn't sometimes!) - Maw tries tae rush the boys past some o' the pictures wi people wi'oot their claes on.

There's special galleries - just portraits - or just modern, but everyone likes something different. Paw's not sae keen on the Modern Art. He looks at ane and says "Weel, it'll be nice when it's feenished, maybe!" Daphne says she likes "The Glasgow Boys".

Now we go again and again, and I keep going back to the same paintings for another look. I've got some real favourites and every time ye look at a painting ye can see somethin' you dinnae see before, that stops ye and makes ye think.

There's plenty space usually, so even if ye're tall or short or cannae see, ye can go close or stand back and take a good look. Ye can go richt close and see the strokes o' the painter's brush.

Granpaw's never talked about art, but he really likes a wander in a Gallery, but what he really likes best is an exhibition of photographs - he likes the auld ones. "Those were the days" he says - aboot everything. The auld days cannae all have been good can they? The galleries have special exhibitions as well as pictures that are there all the time. Exhibitions are usually on for a wee while so there's plenty time tae go, and go back again!

I went to see sculptures the last time. It's amazing what some artists can do with their hands. I'm not so sure about that Turner Prize though. Sometimes I think folk are just havin' a laugh. Maybe if I hung all of Daphne's shoes on a washin' line oot the windae at Glebe Street it would be art.

(i) Galleries not to be missed. These are some of the most popular galleries in Scotland and the great thing aboot them is that they are all free (though sometimes ye'll need tae pay tae see a special exhibition).

Art Galleries

Gallery of Modern Art, Glasgow G1 3AH.
Tel: 0141 287 3050 www.glasgowmuseums.com

The Burrell Collection, Glasgow G43 1AT.
Tel: 0141 287 2550 www.glasgowmuseums.com

Scottish National Gallery of Modern Art, Edinburgh EH4 3DR.
Tel: 0131 624 6200
www.nationalgalleries.org

Aberdeen Art Gallery and Museum,
AB10 1FQ. Tel: 01224 523 700 www.aagm.co.uk

National Gallery of Scotland, EH2 2EL.
Tel: 0131 624 6200 www.nationalgalleries.org

Perth Museum and Art Gallery, PH1 5LB.
Tel: 01738 632488 www.pkc.gov.uk

Hunterian Art Gallery, Glasgow G12 8QQ.
Tel: 0141 330 4221 www.hunterian.gla.ac.uk

Kirkcaldy Museum and Art Gallery, KY1 1YG.
Tel: 01592 583213 www.fife.gov.uk

Dundee Contemporary Arts, DD1 4DY.
Tel: 01382 909900 www.dca.org.uk

Pier Arts Centre, Stromness, Orkney KW16 3AA.
Tel: 01856 850209 www.pierartscentre.com

57

Country Parks

Scotland abounds with country parks, woods, forest and areas of outstanding natural beauty. Many are within easy reach of Scotland's towns and cities, and are free.

Country parks tend to have good paths and are specially managed to make them easier to explore and appreciate. Most have well-marked paths of different lengths and difficulty, and substantial areas where you are free to roam. Natural beauty, wildlife and our cultural heritage are easy to appreciate in them, and the country parks are designed so that we can enjoy and understand our country more. Most country parks are used for walking, dog walking, or cycling and mountain biking.

Country Parks: Information

Volunteering to help

Many of the agencies and trusts that manage woodlands and parks run volunteer events to get you involved, and they encourage volunteers to help make paths and assist with conservation projects, or activities such as being involved in a wildlife watch. The Forestry Commission in Scotland, for example, actively promotes woodlands for healthy exercise, and their website will also direct you to the best places to catch a glimpse of a red squirrel and or a rare bird, such as the peregrine falcon.

More information on country parks, woodlands, forest, areas of outstanding natural beauty and internationally recognised heritage sites can be found on the following websites:

Forestry Commission: www.forestry.gov.uk/scotland
Their properties include Glen Affric, Bennachie, Galloway Forest Park, Queen Elizabeth Forest Park, Glenmore Forest Park Visitor Centre.

John Muir Trust: www.jmt.org
Their properties include Ben Nevis, Schiehallion, part of the Skye Cuillins, properties in Knoydart.

RSPB (Royal Society for the Protection of Birds): www.rspb.org.uk/ourwork/around_the_uk/scotland.asp
Their properties include Lochwinnoch, Inversnaid, Vane Farm (Perth and Kinross), Coll.

National Trust for Scotland: www.nts.org.uk
Their properties include Brodick, Culzean and Crathes Castle.

Scottish Natural Heritage: www.snh.org.uk
Their properties include Clyde Valley Woodlands, Loch Lomond, Beinn Eighe (Torridon).

Woodland Trust: www.woodland-trust.org.uk

Wildlife Trust: www.wildlifetrusts.org

Local authorities: check your local council's website for country parks near you.

UNESCO (international designations, e.g. New Lanark) http://whc.unesco.org

RED SQUIRREL

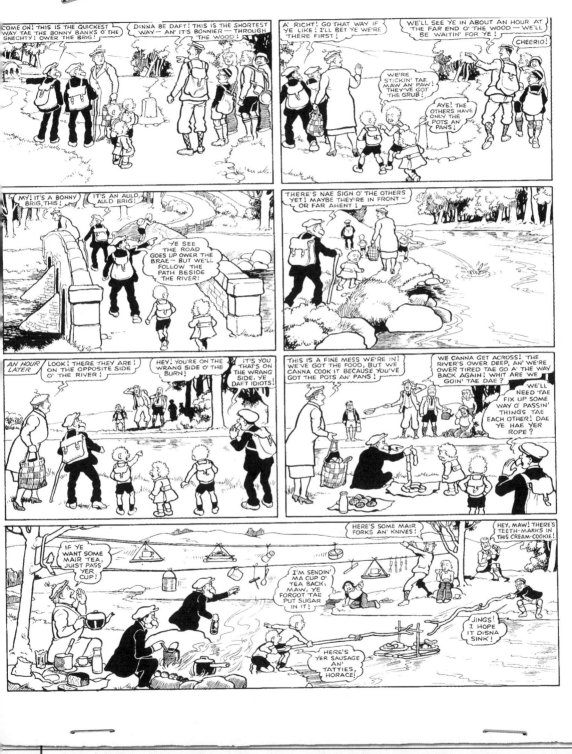

59

Loch Lomond

Loch Lomond is our biggest loch and it's really close tae Glasgow, so lots of us enjoy it. Here's some more aboot it, and some suggestions of things ye can do.

THE BONNIE, BONNIE BANKS...

Loch Lomond is 24 miles long. It is narrow at the top (about three-quarters of a mile wide) and widest at the bottom, where it is 5 miles wide. It is also much deeper towards the top – the deepest part is around 600 ft deep. It is the largest loch in Great Britain. At the northern end it is surrounded by ranges of high mountains - Ben Vorlich, Ben a Chroin and Ben Lomond, while, as it widens towards the south, it embraces a charming group of 30 wooded islands. At Balloch at the southern end of the loch, the River Leven flows south out of the loch and joins the Clyde at Dumbarton, a few miles away.

The loch holds a great number of fish. Salmon and sea trout come back up the River Leven into the southern parts of the loch, and brown and rainbow trout, pike, roach, chub, perch and dace add to the variety.

(i) You can find out lots more about Loch Lomond at:
www.loch-lomond.net
www.lochlomondangling.com
www.visit-lochlomond.com
www.maidoftheloch.com

The Maid of the Loch.

Loch Lomond

Boating on the Loch

Loch Lomond has always had a boating tradition and the loch has been well used by folk wanting to enjoy the area from the loch. The first commercial pleasure steamer started service in 1827. Since that time there has been a steady increase in the numbers and type of craft using the loch.

The Maid of the Loch

At Balloch Pier is "The Maid of the Loch", a paddle steamer that used to work on the Loch and which you can now visit. It was the last paddle steamer built in Britain and is now being restored. Leaving Balloch Pier, on the right bank you can see Balloch Park and Boturich Castle, once an ancient seat of the Lennox family and now a country park.

Loch Lomond Shores

On the left you can see Loch Lomond Shores, where there is a Visitor Centre for the Loch Lomond and the Trossachs National Park, which has lots of information about the loch (and a fascinating woodland path, complete with modern sculpture). There's a modern building that looks a bit like an old castle, now the rather surprising home to a sea-life centre. Then Glen Fruin opens up on your left, while, in the middle of the loch lies Inchmurrin ('grassy isle'), the largest and most southerly of the islands, at the south end of which are the ruins of old Lennox Castle. Both this island and Inchlonaig used to be places of "internment for drunken and insane persons".

Balmaha

To the east of Inchmurrin is the village of Balmaha and, immediately opposite it, Inchcailloch, the "island of old women" - so called from a former nunnery there. This island was the burial place of the MacGregors and the yew trees of this sacred island provided the wood for the fiery cross of "The Lady of The Lake". Rising above Balmaha is Conic Hill – a relatively easy climb to the top and great views of the loch and the line of islands that show the position of the Highland Fault Line.

Ben Lomond

North of the islands you approach Luss picturesquely situated on the west bank, and then, on the east side, is Rowardennan, a common starting point for the ascent of Ben Lomond, the most southerly Munro peak, which dominates the scene. Onwards to Tarbet on the west side and ahead a view up Glen Falloch at the head of the loch.

Rob Roy

At Inversnaid, on the east, the route from the Trossachs comes in. On the rocks to the right, high up, is Rob Roy's cave where Bruce is said to have sheltered in 1306 and a little farther on is Eilean Vow, an islet with a ruined castle of the Macfarlanes. Yews are said to have been planted on the islet by Bruce to provide bows for his successors.

At Ardlui, at the top of the loch, there is a station on the West Highland Railway, another picture postcard opportunity.

WET WET WET DAYS
by Paw Broon

Wet days, days when it's jist rainin' big cats an' Rottweilers. What is there tae dae? Well, oor lot sometimes dae the usual things like goin' tae "the picters" (cinema, folk ca' it now) an' as ye ken, there's nae end o' fine museums and the like for damp days.

But here's OOR favourite wet day oot, well MY favourite actually. It took a bit o' persuadin' wi' the rest o' the gang, but they fair like it tae now. Get oot the wellies an' the waterproofs and jist head oot an' enjoy the weather. That's right, ENJOY the rain. When the Scottish rain has been bucketin' doon for days, head for some o' the maist spectacular <u>WATERFALLS</u> ye'll ever see. Ye mebbe winna want tae walk ower far in the downpour, so jist mak' for the beauty spots a stone's throw fae the road an' yer car. Ye'll never beat the Falls o' Watterytogle aboot a mile doon fae the Linty Loch near the But an' Ben, but that's OOR secret.

Just aff the A9 aboot a mile north o' Dunkeld, look oot for <u>THE HERMITAGE</u>. Park yer car in the National Trust for Scotland car park and follow the wellies in front, under the railway bridge and through the trees. It's no' far, mebbe aboot twenty minutes or so. Soon ye'll come tae what's known as a "folly". It's like a wee hoosie, perched on the edge of a cliff, wi' one side open so ye can look richt doon intae the thunderous waters o' the River Braan. This is ca'd <u>OSSIAN'S HALL</u> and it's spectacular and if ye dinna like this, ye'll no' like onything. Better than a Harry Potter movie and a big bag o' popcorn onyday. And right beside Ossian's Hall there's an amazin' stone bridge spanning the torrent below.

Mair waterfalls? Well, there's the <u>FALLS O' CLYDE</u> at New Lanark and there's the <u>GREY MARE'S TAIL</u> on the road fae Edinburgh doon tae Moffat. When this Mare is in full spate, Cutty Sark hersel' wouldna go near her. <u>ROGIE FALLS</u> between Dingwall and Garve is another belter well worth the effort ony day and richt by the road. And there's the ane I like just ower fae the Inverarnan Inn (The Drover's) at the top o' Loch Lomond, a big white scar on the side o' the hill when its waters are bilin'. The list jist goes on and on. GO AND SEE THEM A'. It could be like baggin' Munros, only it's watter. Maybe someone should mak' up a list.

(i) The Hermitage PH8 0HX.
Tel: 0844 493 2192
Grey Mare's Tail DG10 9DP
0844 493 2249
www.nts.org.uk

A FYNE DAY OOT at INVERARAY
by Daphne Broon

Inveraray, on the shores o' Loch Fyne, is that special ye'd actually think it was built jist for the tourists.

Naebody should come tae the toon withoot visitin' INVERARAY CASTLE, the ancient seat o' Clan Campbell. What a stately pile that is. And what a setting! Hen an' Joe were fascinated wi' the collection o' arms in the great Armoury Room. What is aboot men that mak's them sae fascinated wi' swords an' guns an' the like? There's a display in the basement o' auld cookin' bits an' pieces they once used in the Old Kitchen. I swear I could still smell a big roast o' venison, but maybe it was jist wishful thinkin'. And dinna miss the Clan Room on the 1st floor, wi' its history of Clan Campbell. No' recommended for MacDonalds!!

A quick big bag o' fresh prawns tae eat by the pier and we a' found oorsels in jail. No, we hadna run aff withoot payin' for the prawns! It was INVERARAY JAIL, ane o' the maist unusual tourist attractions ye'll ever visit. It's ca'd "The Living Prison". If that was livin', I'll gie it a miss. There's fowk actin' oot the parts o' guards an' warders, judge an' the like. Ye actually get tae feel what it was like tae be a prisoner. I pretended I'd been locked up for haein ower many boyfriends and pies. Chance wid be a "fyne" thing.

Aboot six miles south o' Inveraray, there's AUCHINDRAIN MUSEUM, a restored farming village, takin' ye back in time in the wee cottages tae a life that the Dukes o' Argyll never knew much aboot in Inveraray Castle. Ane o' the cottages was jist like oor But an' Ben, richt doon tae the pots an' pans an' mangle for the clathes. Maybe we should open the But an' Ben as the Auchentogle Museum, complete wi' Granpaw Broon, the living museum piece.

We had the usual delay settin' aff for hame when Granpaw and Paw discovered the LOCH FYNE WHISKIES shop in the main street in Inveraray. They do hae a fine selection and oor bold lads were in a "fyne" state when they had their whisky tastin'. I'd happily hae locked the two auld rogues up in Inveraray Jail.

Inveraray Maritime Heritage
Museum PA32 8UY.
Tel: 01499 302213
www.inveraraypier.com
Inveraray Castle PA32 8XE.
Tel: 01499 302203
www.inveraray-castle.com

The boats at Inveraray

Alongside the pier in the centre of the town you can see two fascinating old boats. *The Arctic Penguin*, built in 1910 in Dublin, was one of the last iron sailing ships ever built. For 56 years she worked as a lightship. She is now a museum and you can explore all round the boat and find out about the maritime heritage of the west of Scotland.

You can also see the *Vital Spark*. This was not its original name, but it was re-named in 2006 to commemorate the boat of that name in Neil Munro's books about skipper Para Handy and his motley crew, Dan McPhail, Dougie and Sunny Jim, as they sailed around the coast of Argyll. The stories were made even more popular in TV series. The *Vital Spark* is the last working example of a Puffer, boats that went chugging about the West coast for years and years delivering all kinds of supplies. Puffers were a maximum of 67 ft so that they could travel through the Crinan Canal.

WITNESS HISTORY

OPEN ALL YEAR

(i)

Inveraray Jail PA32 8TX.
Tel: 01499 302381
www.inverarayjail.co.uk
Auchindrain Museum
PA32 8XN.
Tel: 01499 500235
www.auchindrain-museum.org.uk
Loch Fyne Whiskies PA32 8UD.
Tel: 01499 302219
www.lfw.co.uk

Inveraray Castle.

Loch Fyne.

Loch Awe and Oban

LOCH AWE AND OBAN

Loch Awe, 23 miles long with an average width of 1 mile, is one of the largest and most beautiful of Scottish lochs, the third largest freshwater loch in Scotland. The head or southern end is comparatively tame, while the foot is magnificently grand. Unusually the loch flows out of the northern end by the Awe into Loch Etive (although a long, long time ago it more naturally emptied out of the southern end towards Loch Crinan).

Cruachan – the hollow mountain

Ben Cruachan, at 3,672 ft, is one of the high mountains at the north end of Loch Awe – but it contains a surprise. Over half a mile below the peak, a huge cavern has been blasted out of the mountain to hold a hydro-electric power station, and what is more, you can actually visit it! A bus takes you from a visitor centre on the banks of Loch Awe, just by the A85 to Oban, into the mountain, and it's so warm there that sub-tropical plants grow.

Kilchurn Castle stands at the head of the Loch - an oblong structure with a square keep. It was built around 1440 by Margaret, the wife of Sir Colin Campbell, the first Laird of Glenurquhay. This castle, a 5-storey keep, faced a siege by Royalists during the Civil War. Later, it was used to garrison Hanoverian troops in the days of the Jacobite Risings. You can get to it from the carpark off the A85 and by following the marked footpath that takes you under the railway line or, in season, by boat from Loch Awe Pier.

In Loch Awe village is the extraordinary **St Conan's Church**. It was designed by Walter Campbell who was not a professional architect but knew what he liked and was able to afford to turn his ideas into reality. It was built between 1881 and 1930, and the result is a magical and moving building. St Conan is said to have been a contemporary of St Columba and is connected with this area.

Bonawe Ironworks In and amongst all this beauty at Taynuilt, on the banks of Loch Etive, are the substantial remains of a charcoal-fuelled ironworks, established in 1753. You can see how iron used to be produced, using charcoal made from the local trees as the fuel.

Kilchurn Castle.

Cruachan Visitor Centre
PA33 IAN. Tel: 01866 822618
www.visitcruachan.co.uk
Bonawe Iron Furnace
PA35 IJQ. Tel 01866 822432
www.historic-scotland.gov.uk

Oban Distillery PA34 5NH.
Tel: 01631 572004
www.discovering-distilleries.com
Scottish Sealife Sanctuary
PA37 ISE. Tel: 01631 720386
www.sealsanctuary.co.uk
For details of cruises, adventure
specialists and watersports:
www.oban.org.uk

Oban.

OBAN

Oban ("little bay" in Gaelic) is the "Gateway to the Isles" - the unofficial capital of the West Highlands. The town's continuing popularity owes a great deal to the Victorians, as the town was a base for visitors touring Staffa and also pilgrims and visitors to Iona (see more about Iona and Staffa on page 70). It is now the ferry terminus for Mull, Colonsay, Coll, Tiree and Lismore; and there are also sailings from Oban to Barra and South Uist in the Western Isles. It is also home to excellent seafood.

Dunollie Castle, an ancient stronghold (12th or 13th Century) stood guard over the narrow entrance to the sheltered bay. It is now reduced to a keep, but is wonderfully situated on a bluff overlooking Loch Linnhe and was originally protected on the landward side by a moat.

The Oban Distillery (1794) is unusual as it is right in the centre of the busy town., but it makes it easy to visit.

On the hill behind the town is McCaig's Folly, an uncompleted circular structure from 1897 which a local banker, John McCaig intended to be a viewing tower, museum and art gallery, but only the outside walls were ever built.

The island of **Kerrera** is a natural breakwater protecting the harbour of Oban. Here Alexander II died in 1249 during an attempt to subdue the Norsemen of the Hebrides. At the south end of the island is Gylen Castle an old Norse fortress - long a MacDougall stronghold.

The Scottish Sealife Sanctuary at Loch Creran is set in picturesque surroundings and hosts a wonderful collection of marine creatures. You can visit the SOS seal rescue facility, and the seal pup nursery, learn about octopus and sharks, rays, starfish, salmon and crabs. There are talks and feeding demonstrations from marine experts.

On Mull

Dervaig.

Tobermory.

The Square, Sale

ISLE OF MULL

Calgary Bay.   AT.1234   M.V. "Columba"

(i)
Caledonian MacBrayne:
Craignure PA65 6AY.
Tel: 01680 812343;
Oban PA34 4DB.
Tel: 01631 566688;
Tobermory PA75 6NU.
Tel: 01688 302017
www.calmac.co.uk

THE BONNIE ISLE O' MULL
Joe Broon

Oh, it's hard tae pick a favourite day oot on Mull. Me an' Hen have cycled the ups and downs of Mull's wee roads that many times and never twa days the same.

Ye can get tae the island on ane o' three different Caledonian MacBrayne boats, and there's nae twa o' them the same. Ane comes intae Tobermory harbour from Kilchoan on the Ardnamurchan peninsula. That's my favourite. Anither crosses tae Fishnish from the mainland at Lochaline and the biggest boat surges over from Oban packed wi' cars and trippers tae Craignure, passin' majestic DUART CASTLE on the way. There's a wee railway runs from Craignure tae the castle. The bairns loved that.

Hen Broon

Joe's richt, it's hard tae pick one day better than anither. But if ye've lang legs like mine (and no' a lot o' folk do right enough) an' ye're a keen cyclist, the single track road from Tobermory past Dervaig, stunning Calgary beach, doon the west past Ulva and Loch na Keal then Salen on the Sound o' Mull and back up the road tae yer start point at Tobermory and a pint is the best bike day oot in the world. It really is. It's less than fifty miles, feels mair like a hunner an' goes up an' doon an' up an' doon.

I've been a' over the world (even tae John o' Groat's nae less!) and this is my number one. Le Tour de Mull. Get yer yella jersey on, mes amis!!

The Twins

Nae cyclin' for us. We just spent the day in <u>TOBERMORY</u>. The hooses on the sea front are a' painted in different bright colours. It's like a scene aff a chocolate box.

The Bairn was in her element, cos this is where the BBC "Balamory" series was filmed. A' the places from the series are easily picked oot. The harbour's packed wi' boats o' every shape and size and on the pier is oor favourite fish an' chipper. Ye'll easily spot it. It's the van parked richt next tae the clock tower in the middle o' the main street. If ye canna spot that, jist look for the big queue, wi' oor cyclin' brothers at the end wi' their tongues hingin' oot.

The Twins

Caledonian MacBrayne

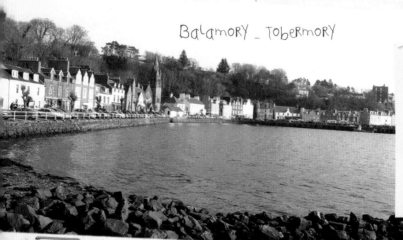

Balamory - Tobermory

(i)

Duart Castle PA64 6AP
Tel: 01680 812 309
www.duartcastle.com
Mull Rail PA65 6AY
Tel: 01680 812494
www.mullrail.co.uk

On Iona

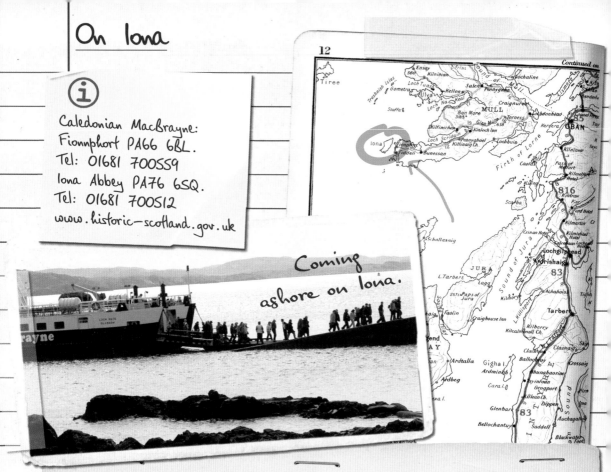

(i)

Caledonian MacBrayne:
Fionnphort PA66 6BL.
Tel: 01681 700559
Iona Abbey PA76 6SQ.
Tel: 01681 700512
www.historic-scotland.gov.uk

Coming ashore on Iona.

Maw Broon

Me and the lassies had only one thing on oor minds for oor trip tae Mull. <u>IONA ABBEY</u> and then <u>FINGAL'S CAVE</u> on the island of Staffa.

I'm no' much o' a history scholar, but I do know a wee bit aboot Iona. (I read it in stuff I picked up at Historic Scotland's reception kiosk actually.) The bonnie wee single track road fae Craignure tak's ye a' the way tae the Iona ferry at Fionnphort. It's only a wee crossing over the Sound of Iona but the wind can blaw a wee bit. I could hardly wait tae get across. Ye can see the Abbey fae the pier.

Iona Abbey stands near where St Columba landed in AD 563. That's no' the day nor yesterday. The place is steeped in history. It was the burial place o' early Scottish kings richt up tae MacBeth in 1057. History tells us that it was the 8th Duke o' Argyll, head o' Clan Campbell, who began the process o' rescuing what was a ruin aboot 1874. And it was Mrs Effie MacDonald that tellt me the Campbell Duke's guid sense almost made her forgive the Campbells for chappin' up her great-great-great-great-great Uncle Lachie MacDonald in Glencoe in 1692. Anyway, what ye see here now on Iona is really a restoration of what was once here hundreds of years ago.

Maggie Broon

I'll better tell ye the rest o' oor wee adventure cos Maw was that impressed she could hardly speak.

It's the boat trip fae Fionnphort tae <u>FINGAL'S CAVE</u> on the island of Staffa. Ye canna really describe it. It tak's yer breath away. The boat will land ye near the cave and ye have tae watch yer step and haud on tae the rails as ye teeter roond and intae the big cave. In some ways it's mair impressive than Iona Abbey inside.

Dinna tak my word for it, just go and see for yersel' . . . and one ither thing, whatever ye dae, dinna miss a wee walk tae see the puffin colony on the north side o' the island while ye're there. It's hard tae believe thae birds are real . . . jist wee comics, like oor Bairn.

PUFFIN

Aww! Look whit the Bairn drew. That's smashin'.

(i)

To find out more about Mull and Iona:
www.explore-isle-of-mull.co.uk
http://holidaymull.co.uk
www.tobermory.co.uk
www.isle-of-iona.com

Iona Abbey.

71

To the Islands

The Scottish islands are some o' the most beautiful places on earth. Even th' tiniest o' them has its own character an' charm. For Grandpaw it has tae be Islay (see page 108), for Joe it's Skye (see page 84), for Daphne it's Arran (see page 38) and for Maw it's Iona (see page 70). Aye, we all have oor favourites. But how tae get there? It's CalMac ye need.

CALMAC FERRIES

Dramatic sunsets, spectacular scenery and a traditional Scottish island welcome are just a few of the things that the network makes possible, whether a trip is a visit to one island or an island-hop round a few.

CalMac sails to 24 destinations on Scotland's West Coast. From Arran in the south to Lewis in the north, the network covers some of the most beautiful and dramatic places in Scotland.

CalMac currently operates a fleet of around 31 ferries to provide passenger, vehicle and shipping services to the islands off the West Coast of Scotland and in the Clyde estuary.

Vast numbers of people get away from it all by ferry with Caledonian MacBrayne and discover a different world, their ferries carrying more than 5 million passengers, 1 million cars, 94,000 commercial vehicles and 14,000 coaches each year.

Islands the ferries go to

Arran	Eigg	Muck
Barra	Gigha	Mull
Bute	Harris	Raasay
Canna	Iona	Rum
Coll	Islay	Skye
Colonsay	Lewis	Tiree
Cumbrae	Lismore	The Uists

Here are some island ideas suggested by Caledonian MacBrayne

Go dolphin spotting
All of the islands are full of beautiful wildlife. Sail to islands such as Arran, Mull or Coll and look out for the mix of wildlife along the way.

Get wet and wild
Tiree is great for windsurfing. Try kayaking in Skye or Uist. Experience outdoor adventure on Raasay.

Go back in time
Discover the history of the islands: Callanais stones on Lewis or whisky heritage on Islay are just a few ideas.

Seek out beautiful buildings
Why not visit the likes of Kisimul Castle on Barra, Kinloch Castle on Rum or Mount Stuart on Bute.

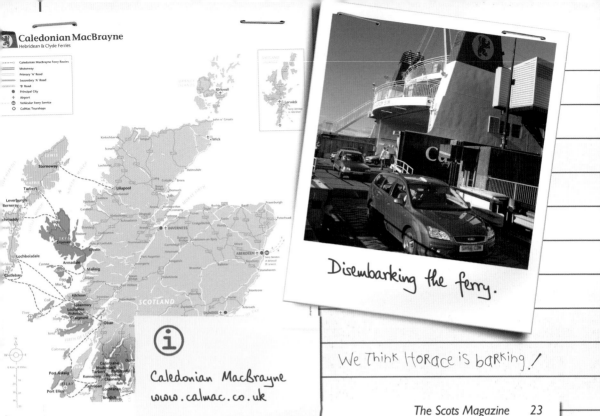

Caledonian MacBrayne
Hebridean & Clyde Ferries

Disembarking the ferry.

(i)

Caledonian MacBrayne
www.calmac.co.uk

We think Horace is barking!

Who are Caledonian MacBrayne?

CALEDONIAN MACBRAYNE started life in 1851 as a steamer company called David Hutcheson & Co and had three partners – David Hutcheson, Alexander Hutcheson and David MacBrayne. The fleet, which David Hutcheson & Co inherited, comprised eight paddle steamers and two track boats on the Crinan Canal. The main sphere of operation, called the Royal Route because Queen Victoria had travelled on part of it only four years earlier, was from Glasgow through the Crinan Canal to Oban and Fort William and then on through the Caledonian Canal to Inverness.

An excursion steamer was based at Oban for Mull, Staffa and Iona and a further vessel sailed all the way round the Mull of Kintyre to Skye. The company, however, extended its operation in 1855 by building new boats for the demanding all year round service to Mull, Skye and Lewis and by extending sailings to Stornoway inaugurated its first service to the Outer Isles.

Throughout the late 1870s and 80s the MacBrayne empire continued to expand with a mail ship to Islay, Harris and North Uist from Skye, and from Oban to Barra and South Uist. It then modified its sailings as the railways came to the coast, and carried on providing its services to the islands.

In 1964 the government provided finance for three new car ferries to link Skye to the Outer Isles, Skye with Mallaig and Mull with Oban and Morvern. Five years later the state-owned Scottish Transport Group was formed to operate not only MacBrayne's but also the Caledonian Steam Packet Company on the Clyde. Soon after they were amalgamated and renamed Caledonian MacBrayne Ltd. The CalMac vessels soon sported the red CSP lion in the yellow disc in the centre of the red funnel. The Head Office was established in Gourock. In February 2001 Caledonian MacBrayne celebrated their 150th Anniversary.

Glencoe

Dark Glencoe by Joe Broon

GLENCOE is ane o' the most popular places in Scotland for climbers and walkers. I've been comin' here for years an' years. There's something for a'body fae the wee Bairns tae the auldest rambler like Granpaw, he himsel' once known as the Rannoch Fox. Folk tell me it was because he kent the Glencoe hills an' Rannoch Moor like the back o' his hand. Masel', I think he got his nickname for scroungin' other folk's cheese sandwiches an' beers in the twa famous hotels, the KINGHOUSE and the CLACHAIG.

The Clachaig Inn has a notice ootside saying 'Nae Campbells', a reference tae the Campbell militia that massacred the MacDonalds in Glencoe in 1692. Ye can find oot a' aboot that at the NTS VISITOR CENTRE just aff the main road a mile or so ootside Glencoe Village. The Kingshouse Hotel sits nestled at the foot o' Glencoe's most popular mountain, Buachaille Etive Mor ('The Great Shepherd of Etive' tae English speakers). THE GLENCOE MOUNTAIN Ski Centre is also just a stone's throw fae the Kingshouse (well, a big stone's throw . . . an Olympic record throw mair like). Even if ye're no' a keen skier like me, ye can still have a trip on the ski lift up intae the hills on Meall a'Bhuiridh. What a view, but mind an' pack yer thermal undies. It's nae place for a real Scotsman in a kilt.

Of course, if ye're a strappin' hill man like masel' there are a' manner o' exciting climbs, including the traverse of the Aonach Eagach ridge that forms the north "wall" of the glen. It featured in a Harry Potter film and Dumbledore's Castle was also thereaboots, but ye either hae tae be a magician or a serious rock climber tae tackle this, so just best enjoy the view fae the road.

"Roond the corner" fae Glencoe, there's the wee village o' KINLOCHLEVEN. It straddles the popular WEST HIGHLAND WAY (the long distance path fae Glasgow tae Fort William) so there's plenty o' places for food an' drink. There's also THE ICE FACTOR, an indoor ice climbing wall that's worth a look-see. It's housed in the auld KINLOCHLEVEN ALUMINIUM WORKS.

After a day oot in Glencoe the best thing tae demolish (massacre even!) is a fish supper fae the chippie in Kinlochleven.

HIGHLAND COACH TOURS

8D FARE STAGE 3

SINGLE

Show ticket on demand from inspector

PRINTED IN INVERNESS X2784

favourite Glencoe walk

walk that almost anyone can manage starts right in the heart of the glen. Park your r in one of the high car parks, just before the ad going east heads into the obvious gorge th a waterfall.

Head down and across the river by a scary idge (children and dogs on a lead!) and then uphill through thriving young native trees d into the LOST VALLEY.

It's a big flat area you would never guess as there and you get no idea of what it's like om the road. It's where the MacDonald Clan putedly kept their stolen cattle. The cattle ust have been very fit, like mountain goats, r it's a steep walk all the way into the Lost lley. The walk is well worth all the panting d sore legs.

There are many forest walks down in the art of the glen near the village. The visitor ntre has all the information you need for ese walks.

Ahh! The shirl o' the pipes. Music tae ma ears!

ⓘ

he Kingshouse Hotel PH49 4HY.
Tel: 01855 851259
www.kingy.com
he Clachaig Inn PH49 4HX.
Tel: 01855 811252
www.clachaig.com

Days Out: Slates of Scotland

RIGHT AT the back of the village of Ballachulish is an enormous slate quarry, that once upon a time supplied nearly all the houses in Scotland. It's not working now but it's a spectacular sight and Ballachulish slates are still sought after for re-use when old buildings are demolished.

ⓘ

Glencoe Visitor Centre NTS PH49 4LA.
Tel: 0844 493 2222
www.nts.org.uk
Glencoe Mountain (ski lift) PH49 4HZ.
Tel: 01855 851226
www.glencoemountain.com
The Ice Factor PH50 4SF.
Tel: 01855 831100
www.ice-factor.co.uk

THE BIG MUNRO, BEN NEVIS,
by The Broons' Mountaineering Club   *4,408 ft – awfy high!*

Hen Broon, team leader

It was my idea tae get the family oot on the highest mountain in Britain. Easy for me of course wi' my long legs. I'm like a mountain goat. But no' sae easy for the likes o' the Twins or the Bairn. Here's a tip . . . there's nae need tae go a' the way tae the summit tae enjoy the day oot. More o' that later.

The Ben sits looking doon on <u>FORT WILLIAM</u> in the West Highlands. There's a good footpath a' the way tae the very top. Easiest start point is from the car park at <u>ACHINTEE</u>. Ye'll find it well marked, but the Tourist Info Office in Fort William will help if ye need it. They'll no' help ye get UP, that's YOUR problem. Best tae get an early nicht and an early start.

We set off at six in the mornin', wi' a'thing we needed in the rucksacks . . . spare waterproof clothes, plenty o' drinks an' enough sandwiches tae feed the Black Watch. Ye need it all!! Even the Bairn an' Granpaw were there. The bigger folk took turn aboot tae gie the Bairn a piggyback fae time tae time. The path is actually easy to begin with, as it angles gently up above bonnie <u>Glen Nevis</u> on yer right-hand side. Ye look doon on the camp and caravan sites and the Youth Hostel, rare places tae spend a few days. Ye'll be amazed at the number o' hills ye see soaring up around aboot.

Now, even at oor "family" pace and a few stops tae drink from the burns, we arrived in good order at the halfway lochan (Lochan Meall an t-Suidhe) at around nine o' clock. This is the secret o' a good DAY OOT on the Ben. Early birds!! Now, it was about here that Granpaw, Maw and the Bairn decided tae picnic an' then mak' their way back doon tae enjoy Fort William, and the Bairn skipped a' the way doon!

Good advice tae remember is that it can snow on this biggest of Munros (hills over 3,000 ft) even in the summer. Check the weather forecast.

ⓘ

Fort William Tourist Information
PH33 6AJ Tel: 08452 255121
www.visithighlands.com
Lochaber Leisure Centre PH33 6BU
Tel: 01397 704359
Crannog Seafood Restaurant PH33
6DB. Tel: 01397 705589
www.crannog.net

ⓘ

Glen Nevis Youth Hostel PH33 6SY
Tel: 01397 702336
www.syha.org.uk

Ben Nevis information: www.
mountainwalk.co.uk/benneviswalk.html

Maggie Broon
Me an' Daphne were near on oor knees at this point, but as the laddies said we'd never mak it tae the tap, we had nae choice but tae carry on. Never make it indeed! Cheek! We just had a wee breather, checked the make-up and the lipstick and set off in the lead. We'd show thae men. (Famous last words).

Joe Broon
At the halfway point, ye can turn left doon past the lochan and head without more climbing roond the shoulder o' the Ben tae the <u>Scottish Mountaineering Club Hut</u> below the vast and REALLY impressive cliffs of the Ben. In some ways, this is a better day than goin' a' the way tae the top. It's the most impressive view in Scotland.

Paw Broon
I couldna let the lassies go on withoot their faither tae look efter them, so I took a deep breath and sauntered on wi' the Twins an' Horace. Horace offered tae carry ma pack, so I let him (just so he wid look the part, ye understand!).

Ben Nevis — continued

Daphne Broon

The path fae the "halfway" lochan to the very top took me anither three hoors. It winds backwards and forwards and backwards and forwards and upward and upward. They tell me the view was braw on the way up, but I had that much sweat pooring doon ma face, the first I saw was at the summit when I wiped ma red moosh wi' Joe's bandanna. I had tae look ma best for this walker fae Paisley wha helped me up the last hunner feet. Erchie Munro, by name, and the best-looking Munro I saw a' day I can tell ye.

The pat

Ben Ne

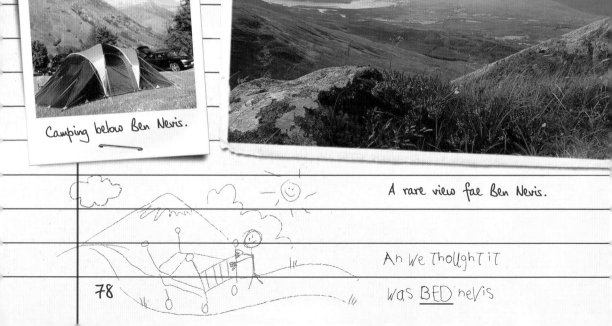

Camping below Ben Nevis.

A rare view fae Ben Nevis.

An we thought it

was BED nevis

78

Out & About: *Ben Nevis facts*

- Ben Nevis is the highest mountain in Britain. It is 4,408 ft (1,344 metres) high.
- In a year twice as much rain falls on the top of Ben Nevis as in Fort William.
- On average, the top is in clouds nine days out of ten.
- The first recorded climb was made in 1771 by James Robertson.
- A bed, a wheelbarrow and an organ have also been pushed to the top.
- Around 100,000 people climb Ben Nevis every year.

- Clement Wragge climbed Ben Nevis every day from 1 June to 14 October 1881 to take weather readings.
- There was an observatory on the summit that was manned all year round from 1883 to 1904.
- There was a Temperance Hotel with four bedrooms at the summit which functioned in the summer until 1916.
- In 1911 a Ford Model T car was driven to the top of Ben Nevis – but it did take five days.

Hen Broon

So there we were, on the summit looking like folk that had run twa marathons, but it was worth it. Ye can literally see for miles in a' directions and richt oot tae the Outer Hebrides on a good day like we got. Ye'll never forget being here if ye can mak' the effort.

Some hill runners can run tae the summit an' back tae Fort William in less than twa hours and it had taen us six just tae get up . . . six hours, 25 stops and four picnics, but what's the hurry? Easy does it. And it was only mid-day. The only anes o' oor team no' oot o' breath were the Twins and Horace. Piece o' cake tae them . . . them that normally canna go tae school withoot gettin' a lift!

And then it was a' doonhill tae Fort William . . a few blisters an' a few aches and pains (well, a lot for some in truth), but WHAT a day oot. We met up wi' Maw, Granpaw and the Bairn who spent the afternoon in the Lochaber Leisure Centre. Efter we'd soaked in hot baths for what seemed like hours, we treated oorsel's tae real seafood in the CRANNOG SEAFOOD RESTAURANT. And Jings! you can fair eat efter a day like that. Paw was that knackered he didna even check the bill!

So, get yer boots looked oot and get oot there. What are ye waitin' for? The Big Ben beckons!!

The West Highland Railway

Hen

THE WEST HIGHLAND RAILWAY
by Hen Broon

Surely the maist famous stretch o' rail track in Scotland. An unbroken ribbon of metal rail a' the way fae <u>GLASGOW QUEEN STREET</u> tae the fishing port of <u>MALLAIG</u> looking across the sea to Skye. It touches the Clyde, Loch Long, Loch Lomond, the vast deer-filled and bog-filled expanses o' Rannoch Moor, Fort William, Glenfinnan and oot tae the sea past bonnie Morar Sands. What an incredible journey!

Of course, the trip fae Glasgow tae Mallaig and back is a day oot in itsel'. Yer nose will be pressed tae the train windae the whole way. It's like lookin' at the best ootdoor TV programme ye've ever seen. But there's so much to see along the way, ye'd be daft no' tae hae as many days oot on this line as yer wallet will allow. I've been up an' doon it for years and still no' seen everything there is tae see. Oh, and there was this bonnie lassie Mary fae Arisaig . . . but that's anither story. I'll just gie ye a quick train ride a' the way fae Glasgow and then come back and fill in a' ma favourite gaps later.

All aboard at Queen Street Station and doon the watter, doon the Clyde, under the Erskine Bridge and intae <u>HELENSBURGH</u> at the foot o' the Gare Loch. Alight here tae see Charles Rennie Mackintosh's The Hill Hoose, sorry House.

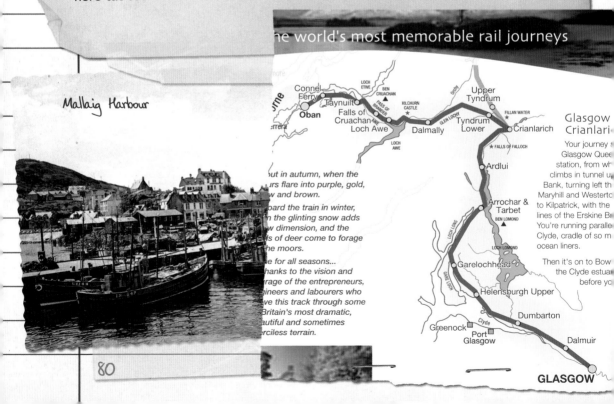

...he world's most memorable rail journeys

Mallaig Harbour

...ut in autumn, when the
...urs flare into purple, gold,
...w and brown.

...board the train in winter,
...n the glinting snow adds
...w dimension, and the
...s of deer come to forage
...he moors.

...e for all seasons...
...hanks to the vision and
...rage of the entrepreneurs,
...gineers and labourers who
...ve this track through some
...Britain's most dramatic,
...autiful and sometimes
...erciless terrain.

Glasgow – Crianlari...

Your journey s...
Glasgow Quee...
station, from wh...
climbs in tunnel u...
Bank, turning left th...
Maryhill and Westerto...
to Kilpatrick, with the...
lines of the Erskine B...
You're running paralle...
Clyde, cradle of so m...
ocean liners.

Then it's on to Bow...
the Clyde estua...
before yo...

Connel Ferry · Oban · Taynuilt · Falls of Cruachan · Loch Awe · Dalmally · Tyndrum Lower · Upper Tyndrum · Crianlarich · Ardlui · Arrochar & Tarbet · Garelochhead · Helensburgh Upper · Dumbarton · Greenock · Port Glasgow · Dalmuir · GLASGOW

Helensburgh

Steaming over Glen...

Spean Bridge
Tulloch
LOCH LAGGAN
Roy Bridge
INVERLOCHY CASTLE ★
LOCH TREIG
Fort William
BEN NEVIS ▲
LOCH OSSIAN
Corrour
BLACKWATER RESERVOIR
LOCH LAIDON
Rannoch
GLENCOE SKI CENTRE ★
RANNOCH MOOR
BLACK MOUNT
Bridge of Orchy
Upper Tyndrum
FILLAN WATER
GLEN LOCHY
Tyndrum Lower
Dalmally
Crianla...

N. R.
Storage
Granton
T? (No.9)
BURNTISLAND
Via Ferry
Not Transferable
...A (S)
...island v F   **OVER**

At Go...
you s...
Ranno...
peat bo...
lochans,...
ancient fo...
Highland W...
to Fort Willi...
moor, but c...
crosses th...
this was a...
'floating...

Crianlarich to Fort William
At Crianlarich, the northbound fork of the West Highland Line

(i) The Hill House, Helensburgh
G84 9AJ.
Tel: 0844 493 2208
www.nts.org.uk

Gare Loch to Rannoch
Now on up the Gare Loch past a' the military bases and oot intae the sunshine on Loch Long and afore long ye'll see the outline of one of Scotland's most famous hills appearing on yer left, the Cobbler. Only 2,891 ft high but a gem . . . and a rock climber's paradise. Loch Lomond comes suddenly into view at Tarbet and if ye're quick, ye'll see Ben Lomond across the waters of the loch on yer right (ye'll need tae be sittin' on the right-hand side o' the train of course, or move folk aside tae get a wee keek).

Scotrail steams on (it disnae really, it's diesel) passing Ardlui and then running alongside the West Highland Way footpath that came up the other side of Loch Lomond. Up Glen Falloch now, past old Caledonian pine trees and into CRIANLARICH under mighty Ben More. Ye can change trains here and head out west tae Oban, but it's over late for that now, for ye've got yer ticket tae Mallaig already paid for.

Clicketty-click, clicketty-click (I love sayin' that on trains) to Tyndrum where the rail track heaves the train uphill and north towards Glencoe. But there's only tantalising glimpses o' Glencoe for me (a bit like Mary fae Arisaig really) and the train swings away north-east from Glencoe and parts company with the West Highland Way as we rattle across Rannoch Moor to RANNOCH STATION.

Rannoch to Glenfinnan

Rannoch Station is in the middle o' nae place, but stunningly bonnie. There's that much wet bog aboot here, parts o' the railway line are floating on piles of wood, so it's a bit like the Rannoch Ferry at this point. From here to Corrour Halt and Tulloch Station, the train really does show you the wild heart of Scotland ye'd never otherwise see withoot walking for miles. Not a car in sight. Just hills and lochs and red deer. And then we're back with the cars and buses alongside the track as we shoot doon past Spean Bridge and intae FORT WILLIAM. At this point, spare a thought for the walkers on the West Highland Way who've come the same distance as yersel' on foot!!

There's usually a wee halt in Fort William before we continue way oot west, past the Caledonian Canal at Banavie (Neptune's Staircase, a series of canal locks on your right-hand side is impressive. Boats on a ladder really). The train inches by slowly here so ye'll no' miss it.

Then it's the Wild West past GLENFINNAN and the visitor centre that commemorates the raising of the standard at Glenfinnan by Bonnie Prince Charlie in 1745. Right across from the National Trust for Scotland centre is a tall tower with a Highlander on top framed by the beautiful view doon Loch Shiel. It's no' Charlie, but lots o' folk think it is. Afore ye reach the station at Glenfinnan, ye cross the world's first viaduct made just from concrete. This is the magnificent viaduct featured in the Harry Potter films with the Hogwarts Express whisking Harry off to school. There is a steam train that runs on the Fort William to Mallaig line in summer, affectionately known, to locals at least, as the Harry Potter Express.

(i)

Glenfinnan Monument
PH37 4LT.
Tel: 0844 493 2221
www.nts.org.uk

Over the Glenfinnan viaduct

West Highland Line the World's Top Journey

In 2009 the West Highland Line was voted the Top Rail Journey in the World by the readers of *Wanderlust*, the magazine for independent travellers. It was the first time the award has been made and over 400 journeys were nominated. The journey was recognised for its breathtaking and varied scenery. The Editor-in-Chief of *Wanderlust*, Lyn Hughes, said, 'Having a Scottish winner for this award is particularly exciting, and shows you don't have to travel far for truly world-beating scenery'. Here are the results:

1   The West Highland Line
2   Cuzco to Puno, Peru
3   Cuzco to Macchu Picchu, Peru
4   Trans-Siberian Railway
=5   Eurostar
=5   Rocky Mountaineer, Western Canada
7   Darjeeling Himalayan Railway, India
8   TranzAlpine, Christchurch–Greymouth, New Zealand
9   Orient Express
=10   Devil's Nose, Ecuador
=10   The Ghan, Darwin–Adelaide, Australia

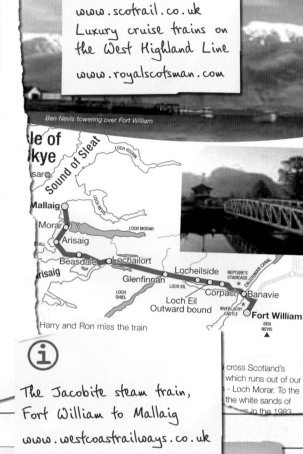

West Highland Line, Scotrail
www.scotrail.co.uk
Luxury cruise trains on the West Highland Line
www.royalscotsman.com

Ben Nevis towering over Fort William

Harry and Ron miss the train

The Jacobite steam train, Fort William to Mallaig
www.westcoastrailways.co.uk

cross Scotland's
which runs out of our
- Loch Morar. To the
the white sands of
in the 1983

And so to Mallaig

The line from here is my favourite bit of railway in Scotland. It just weaves about slowly amongst hills and lochs before bursting out ontae the west coast at ARISAIG and the stunning views of the islands floating on the sea . . . Rum, Eigg, Skye . . . wonderland. Then it's Morar Sands, the quaint level crossing in Morar village itself and the scenic railway stint to MALLAIG and the end of the line right on the sea.

I have to get off here and find some fresh prawns tae eat and then I'm ready for the train back. The fresh fish shop is just roond the corner. Now, I'll tell you aboot a' my favourite walks from the train on the journey back . . . wait a minute, the train's awa'. I'm stranded in Mallaig for the night. But it's no' a' that bad. It's only a wee walk back doon the coast tae Arisaig and bonnie Mary. What was her address again . . .?

On Skye

<u>OVER THE SEA TO SKYE</u>
by Joe Broon

<u>Gettin' there</u>
There are several ways o' goin' over the sea tae Skye.

- Ye can sail in tae Uig fae Tarbert on Harris in the Western Isles on CalMac ferries.

- Ye can drive over the Skye Bridge fae Kyle of Lochalsh tae Kyleakin.

- Ye can tak' "The Road tae the Isles" fae Fort William and CalMac-it fae Mallaig tae Armadale.

- Ye can dae what I always dae . . . fae Shiel Bridge on the main A87 Invergarry tae Kyle road, turn aff at signpost tae Glenelg over the steep pass o' the Mam Ratagan and cross tae Kylerhea on Skye on the wee "Glenachulish" ferry boat. It's the last wee ferry boat o' its kind in Scotland. There's a turntable that the lads push roond by hand so that yer car's aye facin' the richt way for drivin' aff . . . ye'll love this. Do NOT miss it.

There are hunners of books on Skye, so I'm just gonna give ye the driver's (that's me!) tips on oor family day oot birlin' roond Skye in ma wee mini bus.

The Cuillins — daunting!

ⓘ
Glenelg to Kylerhea Ferry
www.skyeferry.co.uk
Information about Skye
www.skye.co.uk

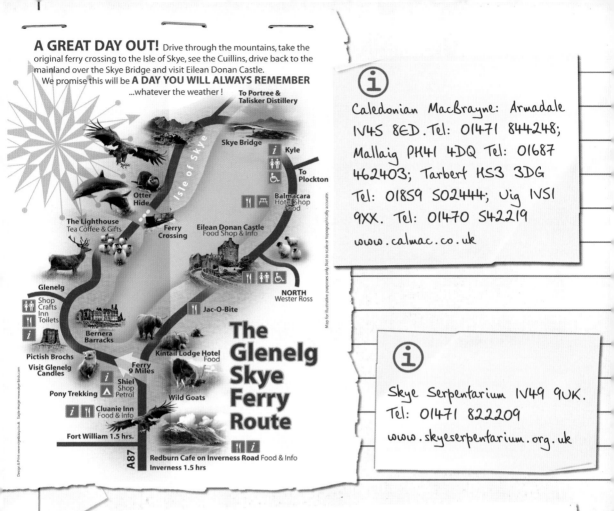

A GREAT DAY OUT! Drive through the mountains, take the original ferry crossing to the Isle of Skye, see the Cuillins, drive back to the mainland over the Skye Bridge and visit Eilean Donan Castle. We promise this will be **A DAY YOU WILL ALWAYS REMEMBER** ...whatever the weather !

To Portree & Talisker Distillery

Skye Bridge

Isle of Skye

Otter Hide

The Lighthouse
Tea Coffee & Gifts

Ferry Crossing

Eilean Donan Castle
Food Shop & Info

i Kyle

To Plockton

Balmacara
Hotel Shop Food

NORTH
Wester Ross

Glenelg
Shop Crafts Inn Toilets

Bernera Barracks

Jac-O-Bite

The Glenelg Skye Ferry Route

Pictish Brochs
Visit Glenelg Candles

Pony Trekking

Shiel Shop Petrol

Kintail Lodge Hotel
Food

Ferry 9 Miles

Wild Goats

Cluanie Inn
Food & Info

Fort William 1.5 hrs.

A87

Redburn Cafe on Inverness Road Food & Info
Inverness 1.5 hrs

Map for illustrative purposes only. Not to scale or topographically accurate.

Design & Print www.sgebuzzy.co.uk · Eagle image www.skyebirds.com

ⓘ Caledonian MacBrayne: Armadale IV45 8ED. Tel: 01471 844248; Mallaig PH41 4DQ Tel: 01687 462403; Tarbert HS3 3DG Tel: 01859 502444; Uig IV51 9XX. Tel: 01470 542219
www.calmac.co.uk

ⓘ Skye Serpentarium IV49 9UK. Tel: 01471 822209
www.skyeserpentarium.org.uk

Kylerhea to Staffin

There's an otter sanctuary at Kylerhea and if ye're lucky ye micht even spot ane o' the bonnie beasts fae the wee ferry itsel'. Even if there's nane there, the mannie on the ferry will tell ye ye've jist missed ane, lookin' the wrang way at the wrang time!! Aye, thae Highlanders!

Up the wee steep road now through Glen Arroch. Feartie passengers on the right side o' the bus. There's a big drap on yer left. We're now headin' through Broadford (the Reptile House, or Skye Serpentarium, for those that like creepy crawlies) then past Sligachan Hotel at the foot o' the Cuillin Hills. Sligachan's the place for climbers an' campers and midges.

We're goin' anti-clockwise roond the island now, cos we're anti-clocks as there's nae great hurry. Coffees an' lemonades an' munchies at the island's capital, Portree (see the bonnie harbour), and a chance for me tae stretch ma legs, afore on and on up the east coast tae Staffin, passin' the Storr Rock on yer left. Cameras oot!!

Dunvegan Castle

Dunvegan Castle
IV55 8WF.
Tel: 01470 521206
www.dunvegancastle.com

Staffin to Dunvegan

Ye can drive a' the way roond the top o' the island and the views are wonderful, but I like tae cut across fae Staffin tae Uig on the ribbon road that climbs up beside "the Quirang". If ye've time, walk up tae see this great pile o' weird and wonderful rock spires. It's like the ruins o' the biggest cathedral in Scotland.

Intae Uig now, where the CalMac boat comes in efter its crossin' fae Harris and we're headed south again. Dinna miss the right turn aff the A856 aboot four miles fae Portree on tae the A850 through Fairy Bridge to DUNVEGAN CASTLE.

This is the home of Clan MacLeod. With pictures of the Chiefs of MacLeod fae the year dot . . . and there's mementoes of that man Bonnie Prince Charlie again and Flora MacDonald, who famously rowed the Bonnie Prince "over the sea to Skye" in song and legend. There's an interesting exhibit at the castle ca'd "The Fairy Flag" from the 7th century. Legend has it that it can only be unfurled three times in case of emergency. It's been unfurled twice already, presumably tae assist MacLeod o' whatever vintage frae bein' attacked by Flora's MacDonald lot. Clans were aye attackin' ane anither. So the flag has only one magic "assist" left. I can tell ye, the MacLeods were nearly bringin' it oot when they saw oor lot pilin' oot o' the mini bus and stormin' the restaurant.

The Cuillins

Then it's doon the road tae <u>TALISKER DISTILLERY</u>, the only ane on Skye. It's aboot here ye get the best roadside views o' the Cuillin Hills, the rock climbers' paradise. Back to Broadford now, retracing oor steps in time for one last Skye treat.

The tiny A881 road runs fourteen unhurried miles from Broadford to another world at Elgol, passing the jaw-droppin' view of the mighty Blaven Hill from a wee place called Torrin. A'body got aff the bus tae photograph this. Doon at the harbour at Elgol is possibly the best view in Skye, lookin' at the whole of the Cuillins like a big oil painting across the sea waters of Loch Scavaig. Sunsets are tae die for here. Ye can get closer on boats like the "Bella Jane", that will take ye right in under the mountains near Loch Coruisk. This is a day oot in itself.

And tae finish aff the rollercoaster day oot in the wee bus? Jist a mile back up the hill, we treated oorsels tae Skye seafood at the Coruisk House Seafood Restaurant. Best tae book though. The braw couple that run the place near choked when The Broons turned up for "a table for eleven". That's a lot o' fresh prawns, lobsters and crab legs and delicious wee things ca'd squatty lobsters. The cook at the restaurant rustled up the Bairn's favourite omelette. Her jaw dropped mind ye, when we asked if she had a "family room". We ran up a rare wee bill, but as Granpaw hadna spent a ha'penny o' his pension since afore the Coronation, it was a painless treat. And as he's sae fond o' his malt, we a' had tae keep him company. Onyway, I'd been drivin' a' day. I deserved it.

Whit a view — magnificent.

(i)

Talisker Distillery IV47 8SR.
Tel: 01478 614308
www.discovering-distilleries.com/talisker
Bella Jane boat trips
IV49 9BJ. Tel: 01471 866244
www.bellajane.co.uk

Loch Ness

ⓘ

Loch Ness (Monster) Visitor and
Exhibition Centre IV63 6TU.
Tel: 01456 450342
www.lochness-centre.com/exhibition.htm
Loch Ness Monster
www.nessie.co.uk

Did you know?

Before the railway was built to Inverness, the quickest way from Glasgow to Inverness was by steamer through the Crinan Canal, stopping off in Oban and then up to Fort William and through the 60 miles of the Caledonian Canal to Inverness. What a great way to travel!

LOCH NESS
by Maw Broon

Nae book aboot days oot in Scotland would be complete withoot mention o' the world famous Loch Ness and its monster.

I've been comin' here since I was a lassie, and in a' thae years, I've never had as much as a glimpse o' the monster in Loch Ness. Mind you, we were ha'en a picnic on the bonnie beach at DORES aye day when a tourist got fair excited aboot seein' the beast. "Look, there it's there . . . ower yonder!" he was yelllin' as he clicked awa' wi' his camera. "Can ye see its lang neck and its black body thrashing aboot in the watter?" I could see what he was lookin' at richt enough, but it was jist oor Hen takin' a photo of Daphne swimmin' in the loch to cool doon.

Dores is a bonnie spot, on the wee road on the "ither" side o' Loch Ness. Ye can drive doon here on the east side o' the loch fae Inverness. Aboot 12 miles doon the same road ye come tae FOYERS. Even at my age I never miss the chance tae walk tae the big waterfall. It's aboot 100 ft high and it's set in the bonniest woodland ye can imagine. In fact, a' roond the loch there are miles o' paths and cycleways through the trees.

Now, as maist folk ken, Loch Ness is part o' the CALEDONIAN CANAL, the famous waterway that splits Scotland fae Inverness on the east tae Fort William on the west coast. And for me, the bonniest part o' the canal is at the south end o' Loch Ness at Fort Augustus. I do like tae sit by the locks and watch a' the boats goin' up an' doon the ladder o' locks. The whole place is buzzin' wi' boats an' chatterin' fowk on holiday. And here's what's braw, naebody is in any hurry. Locks fillin' up, locks emptying, wi' boats goin' up and boats goin' doon. An' there's cafes an' shops dotted aboot the place. I jist love it.

The main road runs up the north shore o' the loch fae Fort Augustus, passin' through Drumnadrochit, whaur ye can visit the Monster Visitor Centre. It's jist past Urquhart Castle. The views are stunning and if ye're no' drivin', keep yer eyes on the loch an' see if ye can spot "Nessie" herself.

The real Nessie got a right fright when Daphne got in the watter.

Loch Ness at Drumnadrochit.

MONSTER HOAX!

The Sunday Post

No. 4506   April 1, 1992   Price 40p

NESSIE SIGHTED!

By A
Sunday Post Reporter

EXCLUSIVE!

See page 10 for more

AMAZING NEW evidence of Nessie, the Loch Ness Monster, was made available exclusively to the Sunday Post this week.

The Sunday Post can reveal the stunning new photo which adds substantialy to the growing evidence that the Loch Ness monster does, in fact, exist.

The crucial picture was taken by Loch Ness fishermen last weeknd and rushed to our offices for publication .

INSIDE: Waether 2,   The Doc 23,   TV and Radio 26-27,   Horoscope 34,   Sport 29-48

■ Last week's Sunday Post cover.

■ Hen Broon's picture of his sister Daphne.

IT SEEMED as though The Sunday Post news team was duped by a holidaymaker whose photograph sparked "Nessie Mania" in the Highlands around the Loch Ness area last week .

Hen Broon aided the Sunday Post in our April fools day hoax which unfortunately led to hundreds of excited calls to our busy telephone switchboard.

The picture in question was simply a silhouette of his sister, Daphne, who was having a dip in the Loch to cool down on what was the hottest day of the year so far this summer in Scotland .

We do hope that all our readers can see the funny side of our practical joke. Watch this space next year!

Urquhart Castle

URQUHART CASTLE
by Horace Broon

Heading down the busy A82 from Inverness along the west shore of mighty Loch Ness, I could hardly wait for my first wee glimpse of Urquhart Castle, and then, aboot fourteen miles doon the loch, there it was. And what a sight. A jagged set of fantastic ruins on an outcrop sticking out intae Loch Ness. Through the bay past wonderfully named <u>DRUMNADROCHIT</u> village and we were there. I near fell oot o' the car wi' excitement.

History tells me this was once one of Scotland's largest castles and I believe it. The Visitor Centre was opened in 2002 and it's built intae the hillside below the main road. Great views of the loch fae here. There's a shop and a cafe of course (isn't there always?) and great audio visuals . . . but what caught my attention was the model of the castle afore folk started knocking lumps aff it. It looks like something frae "Lord o' The Rings" and ye can easily imagine armies stormin' the gates and gettin' their fingers burned fae the defending sojers.

Don't whatever ye do, miss the view from the top of the Grant Tower . . . or what's left of it, that is. I just loved wandering up and down the steps and paths connecting the various parts of the castle that still remain. Ye'll see that the castle was once narrow in the middle as it was built on two separate rocky tops. Ye can also see that well in the model in the Visitor Centre.

So there ye have it, a day oot in bloody Castle Urquhart. I only get tae say bloody now and again, but it's true here. This is a castle tae gladden every schoolboy sojer's warring heart, and mind an' keep an eye on the 600-ft deep still waters of Loch Ness. Who knows WHAT lurks doon there. A monster mebbe? And if IT has a day oot, RUN!!

Urquhart Castle.

Urquhart Castle.

(i)

Urquhart Castle
IV63 6XJ.
Tel 01456 450551
www.historic-scotland.gov.uk

My history of Urquhart Castle

Jist how lang there's been a castle here, naebody is really sure, but my history teacher tells me St Columba passed through here on his way fae Iona tae visit the King o' The Picts in Inverness aboot AD 580. Columba was called to see an auld Pictish nobleman ca'd Emchath at his big hoose at Airdchartdan. Whether this Airdchartdan WAS the original fort on this rocky outcrop we canna say. Mind you, Airdchartdan is aboot as hard tae pronounce as Urquhart, so I'd say the story's true.

I love tae read in my history books aboot "bloody conflicts" and "turbulent times" and this place has seen mair than its share. The castle sits astride the major route through the Highlands and it seems a'body and his brother was keen tae own it by fair means or foul. As a medieval fortress from the 13th to the 17th century it was a case o' "never a dull moment". Edward I of England, known to his chums as the "Hammer of the Scots", stole the keys o' the door aboot 1296 and saw off an assault by us Scots later, and then we took it back and Edward's lot came crashin' back in again. Robert the Bruce broke in and took ower again afore he became King of Scots efter Bannockburn, and in 1332 efter The Bruce died, Urquhart was the only Highland Castle holdin' oot against the Auld Enemy. And then, nae sooner had the English lost interest than the MacDonalds fae the Western Isles came battering at the door fighting again and again against the castle folk.

When the last sojers marched oot in 1692, they blew it up so NAEBODY could have it. What aboot that for extreme measures? Part of the big Grant Tower (the main bit ye still see) crashed tae the ground in 1715 during what was described as a violent storm. A thousand years of history disappeared under the rubble.

A Day Oot Aroond Inverness

Baxters

INVERNESS and Roond Aboot
Granpaw Broon

<u>Inverness</u> is the fastest growin' toon in Scotland and it's hardly recognisable now as the sleepy wee place I first visited as a laddie. Comin' doon the hill on the main A9 road intae Inverness, ye can see the <u>Kessock Bridge</u> above a' the new commercial buildings, takin' the main road across the firth and on intae the Black Isle. It's a rare panorama. As a laddie on a youth hostel tour, I had tae cycle a' the way tae Beauly roond the Beauly Firth and roond first ae firth an' then anither. Now ye can speed past Inverness in yer car and be on yer way north tae Wick and Thurso afore ye ken whaur ye're goin'. That's progress or so they tell me.

Now, comin' doon the hill intae Inverness from the south, ye'll pass the turn off for <u>CULLODEN BATTLEFIELD</u>. Even the maist dunder-heided laddies in my primary school history class a' thae years ago knew a' aboot Culloden, if little aboot onythin' else. I've been tae Culloden many times and now with the new Battlefield Visitor Centre, it's proving to be ane o' Scotland's big tourist attractions.

Lying no' that far north o' Culloden on the shores of the Moray Firth at Ardersier is <u>FORT GEORGE</u>, built followin' Charlie's demise at Culloden. This is the mightiest artillery fort in Britain. It took near 21 years tae build and it never saw a single shot fired in anger. Fort Gorge is almost in its original 18th century new-build condition. It has hunners o' arms and bits o' military equipment and fair bristles wi' cannons. And on a cheerier note, ye can often spot dolphins fae whaur the cannon peek oot tae the Moray Firth.

Tired o' blood and glory and stirrin' tales o' battle? Head along the coast tae Fochabers and visit <u>BAXTERS</u> visitor centre. Baxters is as famous as Bonnie Prince Charlie, its soups and home bakes mooth-wateringly wunnerful. As guid as Maw Broon makes. Mair I canna say. And there's a Kids' Adventure Playground. Goin' tae or comin' fae Fochabers, pop intae ma favourite grocers at <u>ELGIN</u>. "Gordon and MacPhail" have enough different kinds o' single malt whisky tae wet the throats of whisky lovers richt across the world. Their Elgin shop's my favourite "retail therapy" day oot.

ⓘ
Culloden Battlefield IV2 5EU.
Tel: 0844 493 2159
www.nts.org.uk/Culloden

ⓘ
Baxter's Highland
Village, Fochabers IV32 7LD
Tel: 01343 820666
www.baxters.com
Gordon & MacPhail IV30 1JY
Tel: 01343 545110
www.gordonandmacphail.com

Days Out: *CULLODEN*

CULLODEN is where Bonnie Prince Charlie's Jacobite Rising finally ended, his Highland men butchered under the withering fire of the muskets and cannon of the Redcoats led by "Butcher" Cumberland, a son of George II, sent up from London. Less than an hour after it started on 16 April 1746, the battle was over and over 1,000 men lay dead or dying. Bonnie Prince Charlie escaped from the battlefield and headed off into telling, song and legend, faithfully sheltered by the Highlanders whose lives he had helped shatter forever. In the words of the famous song "Will ye no' come back again?"

Charlie didn't. He escaped to France and died a sad old man in Rome, leaving behind a broken way of life.

You can find all this out at the visitor centre and experience what it was like in the centre of the bloody battle in a four-minute film in the new "immersion theatre". It's like you were there in the thick of the battle. Take time to walk through the battlefield itself, visit old Leanach Cottage and stand quietly amongst the Highlanders' graves, the men lying asleep on the field of the last pitched battle on British soil.

ⓘ Fort George IV2 7TD.
Tel 01667 460232
www.historic-scotland.gov.uk

Black Watch sojers at the Fort.

Memorial cairn at Culloden moor.

Birds of Scotland

FEATHERED FRIENDS
by Horace Broon

(i) RSPB www.rspb.org.uk

Scotland is one of the best places in the world to be a "twitcher". That's the funny name for folk that are mad about birds. Now, jist so ye dinna get the wrong idea, we're talking aboot days oot tae see feathered birds . . . no' nights oot like Hen and Joe have tae see "the birds" at The Dancin'!

There are so many great places to go bird watching, ye'd need a hale book or twa tae list a' the guid places and the many different birds ye can spot. Visit the RSPB website to get the latest news aboot Arctic geese or oor wee summer visitors fae the South. I've been to lots of RSPB Reserves and my favourite is at <u>LOCH GRUINART</u> on Islay where ye can see MILLIONS of geese from all over the world in the autumn and crane yer neck for the rasping sound of the Corncrake (no, it's no' a breakfast cereal) in the spring. Throw in the odd Golden Eagle if ye're lucky and that's a day oot in itself tae remember.

Near Aviemore, <u>LOCH GARTEN</u> is the home of the <u>OSPREY</u>. It's no' that long ago that there were nae Ospreys left in Scotland, but that's a' changed now. Ye can watch the magnificent birdies through CCTV at the visitor centre. We were luckier than that when we went tae visit. On the A9 near Pitlochry, Joe spotted ane flying richt alongside oor car on the River Tay. It jist dipped doon intae the watter richt ootside the car windae (in a' that traffic!!) and came up quick as ye like wi' an enormous salmon in its talons. That's what I call fishin'. Nae bother at all. I could hardly believe it.

POST CARD

CORRESPONDENCE   Printed in Gt. Britain

Great twitching here! My best sighting was on LOCH NEVIS near Mallaig, when twa Sea Eagles flew richt over the boat tae Inverie. Michty. What a size. They tell me the wing span can be aboot eight or nine feet wide. That's even bigger than Hen . . . OOR Hen, that is, no' the bird that lays eggs.

The Broon Family
Glebe Street
Scotland UK

A huge Sea Eagle.

The Osprey nest.

Wild Geese.

An Osprey catching its tea.

My other favourite Reserves are at:

VANE FARM near Kinross, where there's lots of bird hides and walking trails on the shores of Loch Leven. If ye're awfy unlucky no' tae spot onything rare, ye'll at least spot the castle in the middle o' the loch whaur Mary Queen of Scots was imprisoned for a year before escapin'. LOCHWINNOCH just off the A737 near Beith, the favourite watering hole of the Bonnie Glasgow Birds (Joe made me say that). FAIRY GLEN near Fortrose (The Bairn loved that, but I think it was jist the name), CULBIN SANDS north of Nairn and INVERSNAID on the east shore of the Bonnie Banks of Loch Lomond.

However, even though ye can visit dozens o' bird Reserves, a great day oot can be had wi' jist a packed lunch and a guid pair o' binoculars. There's naebody locks the doors on oor Scottish birds in the Reserves. Ye'll see them a' ower the countryside and in yer ain gairden. Buy some bird feeders, fill them wi' bird nuts and sit back and watch the feathers fly!

SCOTTISH Wildlife

No.12
FROM A SERIES OF 35
INFORMATIVE CARDS

THE GOLDEN EAGLE

The golden eagle is one of the most magnificent birds of prey in the Scotland. The females are much larger than the males. Golden eagles range across Europe, Asia, N. Africa and N. America. In the UK, they are predominantly found in the Scottish Highlands. These large birds prefer mountainous habitats, although they require large trees or rock faces for nesting. Golden eagles hunt mammals, such as rodents, rabbits and young deer. They also hunt birds. They can remain in the air for hours at a time. Golden eagles can attain speeds of 80 mph. They are resident birds and do not migrate. They have exceptionally good eyesight, and when prey has been spotted, they dive down to seize and kill the victim with their curved talons. Golden eagles mate for life. Pairs normally have territories of up to 35 square miles.

SNOWY OWL

PEREGRINE FALCON

PUFFIN

95

Very Old Places

We Scots, well not always Scots, have lived roond and aboot here for a lang, lang time. Some o' the remains left are so auld (yes, much aulder than Granpaw) that we dinnae really know what they were used for. Here are some of the best and, as Skara Brae is part of a UNESCO World Heritage Site, we should be proud of our ancestors.

The Scots Magazine   21

Skara Brae, Orkney

The Neolithic village of Skara Brae was discovered in the winter of 1850. Wild storms ripped the grass from a high dune known as Skara Brae, and exposed the best-preserved Neolithic village in northern Europe. Skara Brae was inhabited before the Egyptian pyramids were built, and flourished for centuries before construction began at Stonehenge. It is some 5,000 years old. The structures of this semi-subterranean village survive in amazingly impressive condition.

All the houses are well-built of closely-fitting flat stone slabs. They were set into large mounds of household refuse and linked by covered passages. Each house comprised a single room with 'fitted' stone furniture made up of a dresser, where prized objects were probably stored and displayed, two box-beds, a centrally placed hearth and small tanks set into the floor, perhaps for preparing fish bait.

Many items have been excavated, including gaming dice, hand tools, pottery and jewellery. Most remarkable are the richly carved stone objects, perhaps used in religious rituals. The villagers were farmers, hunters and fishermen and, as no weapons have been found, they probably lived a peaceful life until the village was abandoned around 2500 BC. No one knows why. Some argue that it was because a huge sandstorm engulfed their houses, others that its decline was more gradual.

ⓘ

Skara Brae KW16 3LR.
Tel: 01856 841815
www.historic-scotland.gov.uk

Calanais

Calanais, Lewis

CALANAIS comprises a late Neolithic stone ring and associated lines of standing stones. Excavations have revealed that the ring was set up between 2900 and 2600 BC, making it earlier than the main circle at Stonehenge. It has a unique arrangement, with lines of stones radiating in four directions from the ring. The layout of the site, along with many others across the British Isles, appears to have an association with astronomical events, the precise nature of which is unknown.

Between 1000 BC and 500 BC, the stones were covered by peat, and it was not until 1857, when the peat was cut, that their true height was once again revealed. In the landscape around the ring are at least 11 other stone circles and settings that hint at how important the area was to prehistoric peoples. The existence of Bronze Age monuments in the area imply that Calanais remained an active focus for prehistoric religious activity for at least 1500 years.

(i)
Calanais Visitor Centre
HS2 9DY. Tel: 01851 621422
www.historic-scotland.gov.uk

The Blackhouse, Arnol, Lewis

Not prehistoric, but near Calanais, and a unique survivor of an old way of life. For hundreds of years it was the custom in Lewis for man and beast to be housed under the same roof. This thatched blackhouse, built around 1880, is the sole representative of a way of life once so common but now altogether gone. In a blackhouse, animals and people lived in the same building and there was no chimney. Having animals 'living in' had its advantages. It made the house warmer and meant fewer buildings were needed. The smoke rising from the peat fire into the roof also had hidden benefits. It killed bugs, and the smoke-laden thatch made excellent fertiliser for the fields.

The blackhouse has a living room, a bedroom, a byre for the animals and a barn. The peat fire in the centre of the living room was the centre of family life and was never allowed to go out.

Kilmartin Glen, Argyll

THIS IS one of Scotland's richest prehistoric landscapes, with more than 150 prehistoric monuments within a six-mile radius of the village of Kilmartin, Argyll.

Many of the sites are looked after by Historic Scotland, and include carvings, stone circles, cairns . . . and Dunadd Fort, which was a stronghold of Dalriada, the kingdom of the ancient Scots.

On top of the hill at Dunadd, two footprints, a boar and an ogham inscription have been carved into the natural rock. Some think that the carved footprints is linked to the coronation of the kings of Dalriada.

The award–winning Kilmartin House Museum was established to investigate and interpret this internationally important archaeological landscape.

(i)
ol Blackhouse HS2 9DB.
01851 710395
...historic-scotland.gov.uk

(i)
Kilmartin House Museum
PA31 8RQ.
Tel: 01546 510278
www.kilmartin.org

The Vikings

GLEBE STREET SCHOOL PRIZE ESSAY
THE VIKINGS

Well done Horace! Very good.

By Horace Brown

The raids of the Vikings (Norsemen) on the west coast of Scotland began around 792. Between 795 and 806, Iona was attacked at least three times. By the latter date it was clear that the Vikings were a very serious threat to all the established kingdoms of the British Isles. Their paganism added a sinister aspect to what, even by the standards of the time, was appalling brutality.

With little space in their ships to take slaves, they killed men indiscriminately but carried off girls and women. Their language and their customs were equally strange. There is ample evidence that they were found to be utterly terrifying. The monasteries and religious hermitages of the Western Isles had been generally safe since around 617, when St Donnan, abbot of Eigg, and his community were killed by pagan Picts (according to legend, ruled by a queen). They had no protection and the surprise nature of the raids made organised defence very difficult. No one could tell where the longships would strike next.

By the early ninth century, the Vikings were settling in Orkney and Shetland, causing the existing population to take emergency measures, like the burying of treasures in the church on St Ninian's Isle (to be discovered in 1958). There is no record of any Pictish expedition to drive out the invaders. The Picts had a long tradition as seafarers, though their boats were inferior to the Viking longships. Such lethargy is not what might have been expected from a strong kingdom with a long tradition of rule in the northern isles. The lack of response suggests that there was no well-established authority in the north at this time.

Some evidence has been found of local resistance on the islands, with hastily thrown-up earthworks on promontory sites. But, by 820, hundreds of little farming-fishing settlements, with Norse names, were established in the islands. Their new proprietors might have gone off on 'summer raids' but they were essentially farmers with boats. Many of the Pictish islanders moved to the northern mainland and there can be no doubt that many Pictish communities were displaced. The record of Viking behaviour elsewhere suggests that for those who could not leave, the future held the bleak alternatives of slavery or death.

Horace is swotty and spotty

98

Jarlshof

At the end of the 19th century, storms ripped open the low cliffs at Jarlshof, near the southern tip of Shetland. They revealed an extraordinary settlement site embracing 4,000 years of human history. Upon excavation, the site was found to contain a remarkable sequence of stone structures – late Neolithic houses, Bronze-Age village, Iron-Age broch and wheelhouses, Viking longhouse, medieval farmstead, and 16th-century laird's house.

Visible remains from this first settlement include a Bronze-Age smithy, built around 800 BC, and houses with distinctive cells formed by buttresses extending into the living space. The broch (a circular broad tower of uncertain use) now stands to a height of 2.4 metres but was probably much higher; Mousa Broch, 10 miles to the north, still stands 13 metres high. The broch was soon joined by other dwellings, including a large aisled 'roundhouse' and a byre.

During the first centuries AD, the broch collapsed to be replaced by structures called wheelhouses because their roofs were supported on radial piers, like the spokes of a wheel. Vikings from Norway settled at Jarlshof in the 9th century. The longhouse forming the heart of the farm is still clearly visible. The farmstead expanded and contracted over

time – some 12 to 16 generations. By the 13th century, it had been replaced by a farmhouse, with barn and corn kilns attached.

Shetland passed from Norway to Scotland in 1469, and came under the control of Earl Robert Stewart. His son, the tyrant Earl Patrick, built 'the Old House of Sumburgh' that dominates the site. The name 'Jarlshof' (earl's house), though it sounds old, was actually created by Sir Walter Scott, in his novel *The Pirate*.

> (i)
> Jarlshof ZE3 9JN.
> Tel: 01950 460112
> www.historic-scotland.gov.uk
> Information about Up-Helly-Aa
> www.uphellyaa.org

Battle of Largs

The battle took place between 30 September and 4 October 1263 at Largs, on the Ayrshire coast. At that time King Haakon IV of Norway controlled Shetland, Orkney and the Hebrides down into western Argyll. Haakon's fleet of longships had anchored off Largs and were badly damaged in a storm. A series of skirmishes with the Scots arose along the shore over a number of days. Eventually Haakon had to withdraw and the fleet broke up. Haakon died on Orkney in December and his son, Magnus V, agreed to hand the Hebrides and the Isle of Man to the Scots under Alexander III. And so it came about that the seaside town of Largs played a key part in making the west coast of Scotland Scottish.

Visit the Vikingar! exhibition at Largs to find out more.

The Sunday Po

Out & About: *Nardini's*

TODAY LARGS is a lot more famous for its ice cream than for its Vikings. In 1890 Rosa and Pietro Nardini established a thriving ice cream shop in Paisley, and their children, decided to move the business to Largs to provide ice cream to all the Glaswegians who went "doon the watter" for their holidays.

In 1935 they built a new cafe on the Esplanade in Largs – and the splendid Art Deco building is still there, bringing back the glory days of the town. It has recently reopened after a major restoration and it continues to serve ice cream – well, 32 different varieties from Vanilla to Scottish Tablet and Peach And Passion Fruit Cheesecake. And there is fish and chips, and an Italian bakery and pizzas . . . Perhaps this is what the Vikings were fighting to get to, with good reason!

> (i)
> Nardini's KA30 8NF.
> Tel: 01475 675000
> http://nardinis.northcolour.com

---

ays Out: *Up-Helly-Aa*

eflecting Shetland's Viking
ions, an amazing festival of fire
d Up-Helly-Aa is held in Lerwick
e last Tuesday in January. The
rations are presided over by
uizer Jarl, who dresses as a
from Norse mythology. There
rch-lit procession of Guizer
s(representing the Vikings) and
ng galley is pulled through the

streets. At the end of the procession the torches are thrown into the galley which then burns. After the burning of the galley there are parties at a dozen halls in the town until the morning and each squad of Guizers have to perform at each hall. It's a long night of celebration!

The Cairngorms

AVIEMORE and ROTHIEMURCHUS

by Horace Broon

I first discovered this bit o' the country wi' the Boy Scouts, but it's really popular wi' folk o' all ages. It's fabulous. Ye'll see walkers and bikers o' Granpaw's age and as young as oor Bairn at every turn in the track here. And now, of course, it's all part of the CAIRNGORMS NATIONAL PARK, so ye have to respect the countryside and no' drop litter or cut doon trees and the like.

I like tae arrive on the train as it drops you right in the middle of AVIEMORE at its bonnie wooden station. After you get yer supplies, hire a bike (or bring yer ain, of course). There are miles of safe places tae cycle wi' the family here and good camp sites, the one at GLENMORE/LOCH MORLICH (four or five miles along the B970 from Aviemore) being aboot the biggest I've seen. There's wind-surfing and boating and kayaking at Loch Morlich and the maist fantastic sandy beach this side of Torremolinos.

If yer legs are up tae it, ye can bike from here a' the way tae the end of the road at COIRE CAS car park, where the funicular railway will whisk you right tae the highest restaurant in Britain, the Ptarmigan, nearly at the top of CAIRNGORM itself (4,084 ft high). Needless to say, the views are immense. Don't forget your camera.

If cycling's no' yer cup o' tea, there's a regular bus from Aviemore to the ski car park. But for me, the treat is to freewheel on my bike doon, doon, doon from the mountain for miles and miles and the canny ride past Loch Morlich and ROTHIEMURCHUS FOREST (what a great name !!) back to Aviemore and the train, or if ye're lucky, a night in one o' the braw hotels or guesthouses. Or camping wi' the Scouts like me.

At Coire Cas, you are in the middle of a winter playground. On snowy winter days, the place is thronged with skiers and snowboarders. If you're not up to skiing, just be like The Broons and bring along a couple of sledges. There's lots of safe areas to pretend you're still young at heart. Granpaw and the Bairn are the Glebe St sledging champs.

ⓘ

e Ptarmigan Restaurant and
airngorm Funicular railway
22 1RB. Tel: 01479 861261
www.cairngormmountain.co.uk
Rothiemurchus Estate PH22 1QH.
el: 01479 812345
www.rothiemurchus.net

24   *Cairngorms / Coire Gas*

Days Out: *Our Favourite Cycle Ride*

■ Head out on the cycle track beside the road to Coylumbridge, the B970.

■ Turn off after Inverdruie and follow the signs for Loch an Eilein. It's an easy cycle run.

■ At the loch, there's an information kiosk and you can cycle round the loch on the track.

The old Caledonian pine trees here are wonderful and the sweet smell of the pine needles in the summer sun is amazing. Keep your eyes peeled for big ant hills, too.

The ants just love making these big stacks with the millions of pine needles.

There's an island in the middle of the loch with a ruined castle that was once the home to a man called the Wolf of Badenoch, the bad grandson of Robert the Bruce (the Wolf burnt down the towns of Forres and Elgin).

You'll love this spot, with its backdrop of the big Cairngorm Mountains and trees, trees and more trees.

Funicular facts

● The building of the funicular started in 1999.
● It opened on 23 December 2001, 40 years after the first chair lift opened.
● It cost around £14.8 million.
● It is about a mile and a quarter long and goes up nearly 1,600 ft.
● It carries 120 passengers (standing) or 60 (seated).
● It takes 4 minutes (winter) and 8 minutes (summer – slower to see the view).
● Steepest gradient is 40 per cent.
● Powered by electric motors at the top and bottom.

ⓘ

Information about Aviemore
www.visitaviemore.com
Cairngorms National Park Authority
PH26 3HG.
Tel: 01479 873535
www.cairngorms.co.uk
Glenmore Campsite PH22 1QU.
Tel: 01479 861271
www.forestholidays.co.uk

The Funicular is piped in.

SCOTTISH **Wildlife**

No.12
OM A SERIES OF 35
FORMATIVE CARDS

GOLDEN EAGLE

GOLDEN EAGLE

Camping

A NICHT OOT CAMPING   by Paw Broon

Now here's a real treat. No' a DAY oot but a NICHT oot, as Granpaw used tae say, "under canvas". There's nae end o' things tae dae and it's a nicht oot ye'll never forget. Ye micht never want tae go on anither ane, but there's mair guid than bad.

If ye're lucky and can find a big open space in the countryside, like we do, near the Lintie Loch at Auchentogle, ye can mak' a big campfire. There's nuthin' as tasty as tatties roasted on a stick on an open fire. Organised camp sites are no' keen on campfires. They have a point I hae tae admit. But ye can jist as happily barbecue sassidges and burgers an' spare ribs an' chops on wee disposable barbecues. Ye'll find lots o' things tae tempt the al fresco (that means no' in yer hoose) chef in Maw Broon's Cookbook.

Now here's guid advice fae someone who knows aboot thae things . . . dinna leave onything behind at the hoose in terms o' food and drink (bein' ootside ye'll need mountains o' things tae shovel doon yer throat!) and dinna leave onything behind like litter when ye leave. Jist bring awa' yer memories.

When ye get tae yer camp site, pit the tents up and mak' doon the beds for later. Ye'll need lights on yer picnic tables of course so ye can see what ye're daein'. Big candles are fine unless it's windy and they keep blawin' oot.

Candles are handy mind, tae keep awa' (whisper it) the dreaded midges. Midges just love campers. Midges dinna need lights, beds OR candles tae hae a guid nicht oot. They jist need you. And there's nae "bein' ower fu' tae eat ony mair" at a midges' picnic. They'll jist bite ye a' nicht if ye let them. So that's anither essential, midge repellent. I find a wee dab o' single malt ahent the ears works wonders.

So there ye are, oot there in the wilds, yer bellies fu', yer beds ready ony time ye feel like it and ye can sit back an' hae a campfire sing song and hopefully watch the embers fae yer campfire float aff up intae the night sky. Ye canna buy that.

And that's aboot it....and ye'll find there's a guid camp site no' that far fae ony place in Scotland.

List o' things tae tak camping
tent...or two or three tents in our case
Sleeping bags
warm clothes
waterproofs
plates, mugs, cutlery
pots and pans fae the hoose an'
camp cooking stoves
disposable barbecues

midge repellent
food
drink
candles
torches
picnic table

Highland Wildlife

No, not Joe and Hen up some Ben, but som advice aboot the wild animals that live in t hills — and where ye can see them avoidin' the climb.

The Wildlife of Scotland (with ma thanks tae Visit Scotland)
By Horace Broon

In an unspoilt area with a low population, there is plenty of room for wildlife, which means the Scottish Highlands provide ideal habitats for a wide range of birds and beasts. In fact, unless you travel with your eyes shut, you are sure to encounter some special creature. Best of all, you don't have to tramp for miles to enjoy exciting wildlife views. Red kites, for example, are easily seen from the car as you travel through the Black Isle north of Inverness while ospreys are everyday birds in the Cairngorms National Park and elsewhere.

Red deer, Scotland's largest wild creatures, also abound in the Highlands and can often be seen from the road, especially in the cooler months when they move down from the high tops.

Another creature closely associated with this area is the golden eagle. Its home is the high moors, crags and mountain corries in many parts of the area. If you are very lucky you may also encounter the spectacular sea eagle in a few places on the west coast, where they have been successfully re-introduced.

There are also lots of places where wildlife spotting uses modern technology to provide unrivalled views of various species such as red kites, ospreys and hen harriers. At Boat of Garten, for example, discreet cameras allow you to watch the activities in the ospreys' nests at close-quarters.

From dramatic sea-bird colonies to pine martens and reindeer, the Highlands offer fantastic wildlife displays.

(i)

Highland Wildlife Park PH21 1NL.
Tel: 01540 651270
www.highlandwildlifepark.org
Cairngorm Reindeer Herd
PH22 1QU.
Tel: 01479 861228
www.reindeer-company.demon.co.uk

The Cairngorm Reindeer Herd

This herd is Britain's only herd of reindeer, found free ranging in the Cairngorm mountains in Scotland. These extremely tame and friendly animals are a joy to all who come and see them. There are currently around 150 reindeer, approximately 50 of them ranging the Cairngorm Mountains and the remainder on the Glenlivet Estate; the locations being some 30 miles apart. There is a daily visit to the reindeer, weather permitting, starting from the Reindeer House at Glenmore, near Aviemore. During the winter months, the visit may be dependent on whether they can be found - they say they're free-ranging and they mean it! Under the supervision of trained guides, visitors can feed and stroke the reindeer.

The Highland Wildlife Park

The Highland Wildlife Park at Kincraig, near Aviemore, is run by the same people who look after Edinburgh Zoo (see page 16), so they know how to do things well and look after all the animals.

At the Wildlife Park, you can discover the amazing variety of wildlife found in present day Scotland, such as the pine marten, wildcat, otter and capercaillie - then step back in time and meet the creatures that roamed the earth hundreds, even thousands of years ago - the animals of your ancestors, such as wolves, lynx, reindeer and wild horses.

The Highland Wildlife Park has expanded its species collection further afield to include endangered animals from the world's mountain and tundra regions. Already home to snow monkeys, red pandas, yak and Amur tigers, the Park will also soon welcome camels and snow leopards!

Drive around the Main Reserve in your own car and then investigate the walk-round area by foot. Throughout the day animal wardens give feeding talks on some of the many creatures in the walk-around area. Watch as some of the animals are fed and hear some more fascinating facts about them!

Distilleries

<u>THE WATER OF LIFE</u> (a day tae remember or maybe not)
by Granpaw Broon

Uisge Beatha, the water of life, amber nectar, call it what ye will, <u>WHISKY</u> has been Scotland's great international symbol since lang afore Irn Bru was ever thought aboot. Ma laddie said he'd write aboot a great whisky day oot, but he's still a youngster when it comes tae bein' a whisky expert . . . no' like masel', wha's been tipplin' the "hard stuff" (in moderation, of course) since afore Paw Broon was a twinkle in ma eye. I do mind "wettin' his heid" wi' a fine wee Laphroaig way back in . . . och, I canna mind, it's that lang ago.

Let's start off oor day wi' folk that'll be able tae explain the magic o' the dram, near Forres, just east alang the road fae Inverness and Nairn. Run by Historic Scotland, <u>DALLAS DHU</u> distillery is a whisky museum, well signposted off the A96 fae Inverness tae Aberdeen. There's nae whisky distilled there nowadays, but ye can still buy "the cratur", the last Dallas Dhu being distilled in 1983.

Dallas Dhu was the last distillery tae be built in the 19th century in Scotland and one o' the first tae be built wi' the pagoda chimney that soon became common on nearly all the distilleries makin' Scotch. While ye're there, visit the visual presentation wi' the free audio guide . . . and the <u>free DRAM!</u> Canna ask fairer than that.

An' dae ye ken, Scotland still produces mair whisky than any other country in the world? As well as bein' oor national drink, it's loved by folk fae Alaska tae New Zealand. So now ye ken how it's made, I'll let ye intae the secret o' how it's enjoyed. And then ye'll be able tae hae braw days oot and many nichts in, savouring the malts o' Auld Scotia. I'll be tellin' ye a' this for FREE, so pay attention. I'll no' be tellin' ye again.

ⓘ

Dallas Dhu Distillery
IV36 2RR
Tel: 01309 676548
www.historic-scotland.gov.uk

Scotch whisky

Scotch whisky, or 'water of life' as it is called in Gaelic ('uisge beatha'), is whisky made in Scotland. It can only be called Scotch whisky if it is made at a distillery in Scotland from water and malted barley, to which only whole grains of other cereals may be added, and it must be stored in oak casks for over three years. The main type of Scotch whisky sold around the world is blended Scotch whisky. There are two main categories of whisky: single malt and blended. Single malt Scotch whisky means the whisky comes from one distillery only, and blended Scotch whisky means that the whisky is composed of malt whiskies from a number of distilleries, and also contains some Scotch grain whiskies.

The first written records of Scotch whisky date from 1494. The ancient Celts knew how to brew, and probably got their skills in distilling from Ireland. Distilling is a craft.

Scotch whisky is made from a mash of cereal grains, which when it ferments with the addition of yeast, produces alcohol and carbon dioxide. This is then distilled. The majority of Scottish malt whisky distilleries use double distillation. There are distinct distilling regions in Scotland, and it is their natural characteristics that help give each region its particular flavours. Speyside, for example, is home to two-thirds of Scotland's malt whisky distilleries, due to the quality of its soft water. Colour is normally imparted to whisky while it is matured in casks. The casks used are made of oak, and are usually ex-sherry or ex-bourbon casks.

Quality whiskies

There's different areas and kinds o' malt whiskies as far as I mind, Island, Highland, Speyside, Lowland, Islay and Campbeltown. But there's only really twa kinds o' whisky . . . guid and better still. But here's ma expert opinion. There's that much keech (no' a word ye'll find in the dictionary - it means somethin' like bird droppings or the stuff ye bag efter yer dog's done its business) talked aboot whisky, it wid put ye aff drinkin'. Here's ane I read no' that lang ago, "10-year-old Glentammynoorie has a long finish, lingering, with hints of old socks, seaweed, warm tarmac, dark chocolate and notes of dandelions. Superb." Superb? Wha's kiddin' wha? Onythin' tastin' like that wid pit a mannie aff his mince. So, jist ignore a' the experts an' taste them til ye find ane ye like.

- Speyside has lovely smooth drams, anes ye'll enjoy if ye're watchin' the rugby at Murrayfield.
- Highland anes wi' a bit mair bite for a day oot in yer kilt.
- Island malts like Highland Park (fae Orkney) and Talisker (fae Skye), perfect for a day oot in yer boat.
- Lowland malts jist rare for a' yer family (over eighteen!!).
- Campbeltown drams like Springbank are Maw Broon's choice. Need I say mair?
- Then there's the peaty Islay giants, Granpaw Broon recommended. To find oot mair, turn the page . . .

ISLAY WHISKY TOUR

And here IS the perfect day oot.

Get the CalMac boat fae Kennacraig tae Port Ellen on the island of <u>ISLAY</u>. It's a lovely crossin', an' as ye approach the island, watch oot for the white distilleries peekin' oot fae their sheltered spots alang the Islay coast . . . names tae mak' yer mooth watter - Ardbeg, Lagavulin, Laphroaig - and then the boat's intae Port Ellen.

Me, I get aff the boat wi' ma auld bike and then cycle (fester then ye'd think!) oot tae the visitor centre at Ardbeg (buy an Ardbeg cycle shirt!!). This dram's ma unashamed favourite and last time I was there, I had a bite tae eat . . . clootie dumplin' wi' Ardbeg.

Now, if ye've guid legs, ye can cycle a' roond the island visitin' Lagavulin, Laphroaig, Bowmore, Bruichladdich, Bunnahabhainn, Caol Ila and twa new anes at Port Charlotte and Kilchoman. There's no' visitor centres at them a', but go onyway.

(i)

Caledonian MacBrayne:
Kennacraig PA29 6YF.
Tel: 01880 730253;
Port Ellen PA42 7DW.
Tel: 01496 302209
www.calmac.co.uk

Islay Whisky Society
www.islaywhiskysociety.com

Stencil writin' on a barrel.

ⓘ

Scotch Whisky Association
www.scotch-whisky.org.uk

<u>And here's how tae enjoy it</u> . . . get yer pals and find a wee hoose like the But an' Ben or a wee cottage or bothy wi' an open fire, wi' wood or peat. Get candles. Pour everybody a guid dram o' Ardbeg. Cup the glass in yer hand tae warm it a bitty and pit yer nose in it. Lovely. Nae hints o' tarmac or auld socks here. Jist whisky. No, no, hae patience, dinna drink it yet. Look at yer bleezin' fire through the whisky in yer glass and watch it dance, smell it again and then tell tales wi' yer auld cronies aboot yer first girlfriend or yer days when ye were near picked tae play for Scotland. We're nearly there now . . . in a wee bit o' quiet, raise yer glass, toast yer auld cronies and doon she goes . . . oh, man, is that guid or what!! Then fill the glasses again.

Slainte! Ye'll no' find a better day oot.

<u>"Should auld acquaintance be forgot an' never brought tae mind . . ."</u>

Royal Deeside

AT BALMORAL
by Maggie Broon

I've aye wanted tae be the Queen. And as that's no' likely tae happen (but I was once the carnival queen), the next best thing was tae be invited tae tea with Her Majesty and get a' dressed up. But that's no' likely tae happen either. So I had tae settle for a day oot in Her Majesty's hoose. Actually, I had tae pay tae get in, alang wi' the rest o' the family, no' the Royal Family, jist oor lot fae Glebe Street. We had a day oot tae Royal Deeside and oor first stop was <u>BALMORAL CASTLE</u>. We drove alang the course o' the River Dee fae Aberdeen. This is such bonnie countryside.

Balmoral Castle sits on the banks of the Dee with "Dark" Lochnagar, the mountain, towerin' up oot o' its back garden. Actually, Lochnagar wisnae dark at a' when we were there. It was bathed in sunshine. The castle was bought by Queen Victoria in 1848 and has been the Scottish home of the Royals ever since. Good Queen Vic's man, Prince Albert, added an extension to the castle made oot o' gleaming white marble fae a local quarry. Apparently 'Bert didna think there was enough room for them in the original castle. He wouldna have been much good in oor wee tenement flat. I jist loved wandering aboot inside the castle, knowing that I was walking through the places the Queen ca's home.

I was in my element in the Castle Ballroom. I jist imagined myself a' dressed up for the ball and the Prince makin' straight for me and sayin', "Miss Broon, will you do me the honour of having this dance?" I would have accepted tae. Granpaw said he used tae go tae dances in a place called Mar Lodge just up the road in what he called the Stag Ballroom. There were stags' heads all over the ceiling and walls. When the Highland dance got goin' the hale place shook and the teeth used tae fall oot o' the old stags' heads and fowk wid slip on them. Trust him tae remember some story aboot teeth fa'in oot.

The castle's only open from the beginning of April until 31st July (it's closed in August, September and October when the Queen and her family are bidin' there and during the winter). But if she's readin' this, I would still like an invitation for ma tea!!

(i)

Balmoral Castle
AB35 5TB.
Tel: 01339 742534
www.balmoralcastle.com

OLD BRIDGE OF DEE.   A.634

Aw, that's awfy pretty.

BALMORAL CASTLE   A.2348

CRATHIE CHURCH   A.2348

111

Aberdeen

ⓘ

Codona's Amusement Park
AB24 SNS
Tel: 01224 595910
www.codonas.com

THE NORTHERN LIGHTS - OOR DAY OOT IN ABERDEEN

by The Broons Twins

We got tae pick this day oot. It was great an' we canna wait tae go back again.

It's the oil capital o' Europe or so Paw tellt us. Ye canna see ony oil rigs of course, cos they're a' offshore in the deep North Sea. But ye can see a' the boats in ABERDEEN HARBOUR that supply the offshore rigs. Walkin' roond the harbour is fascinatin'. There's boats o' every shape and size. Oor favourite was the ferry boat fae Shetland that lands in Aberdeen. It's a lang sailing and the passage over the Pentland Firth can "be a bitty rough" as an auld Aberdonian put it. It was just unloading when we passed and we've never seen sae many green faces in oor lives. We would have paid tae see them.

We didna get things a' oor ain way and Maw and the lassies insisted we visit the shops in UNION STREET. Thankfully, she didna mean a' the shops as this has got tae be the langest street in the world. Aberdeen looks as if it was just built last month. A' the buildings are built wi' granite. It's a local stone that disnae wear at a' it seems. Everything looks new. We liked the big Marischal College. It's an old university building and it's the second biggest granite building in the world.

And now we were aff tae what WE really wanted tae see. CODONA'S AMUSEMENT PARK, right doon on the beach. What could be better? When the weather's good, ye can lie on the sands, hae a swim and head off intae the amusement park. When ye're oor age, nuthin' could be better. There's too many things tae list, but we loved the Pirate Island Adventure Golf. It's 18 holes and it looks like ye're in Florida. Pirates galore and even a big pirate ship . . . and there's a second 18-hole Congo INDOORS jungle golf course wi' jungle trees, tree huts, a big waterfall and an eruptin' volcano. Then there's the Disco Waltzers (haud on tae yer stomach!) and the Super Dodgems. The Bairn loved the Safari Kiddies Train. If ye're willing tae "shoot the rapids" and ye dinna mind gettin' soaked, try the White Water Log Flume. Couldna get enough o' that, and there's Ten Pin Bowling, a huge super slide . . . and . . . and then we ran oot o' time. It was tea time.

ⓘ

The Twins were too busy on the beach tae visit the great hands—on science centre: the Satrosphere on Constitution Street AB24 5TU.
Tel: 01224 640340
www.satrosphere.net

The Ashvale

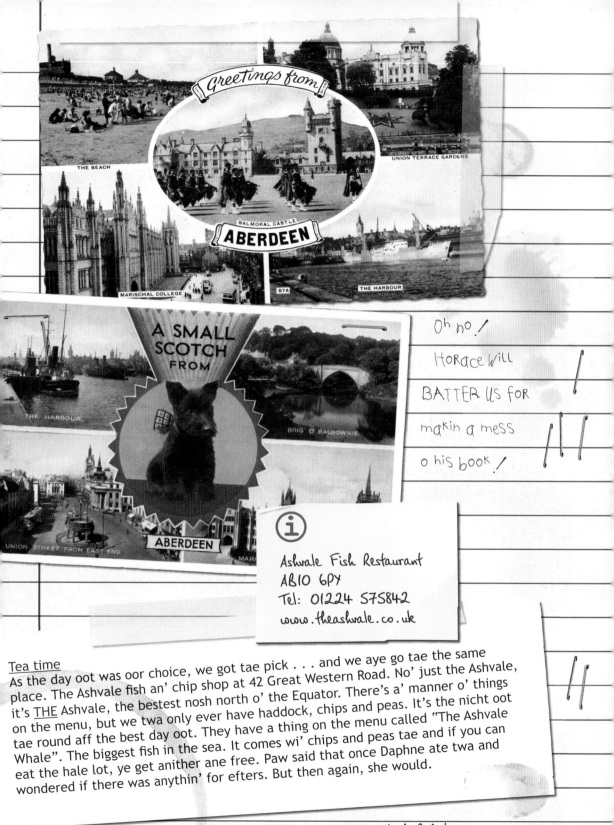

Greetings from **ABERDEEN**

THE BEACH · UNION TERRACE GARDENS · BALMORAL CASTLE · MARISCHAL COLLEGE · B7A · THE HARBOUR

A SMALL SCOTCH FROM **ABERDEEN**

THE HARBOUR · BRIG O' BALGOWNIE · UNION STREET FROM EAST END

Oh no!
Horace will
BATTER US FOR
makin a mess
o his book!

(i) Ashvale Fish Restaurant
AB10 6PY
Tel: 01224 575842
www.theashvale.co.uk

Tea time

As the day oot was oor choice, we got tae pick . . . and we aye go tae the same place. The Ashvale fish an' chip shop at 42 Great Western Road. No' just the Ashvale, it's <u>THE</u> Ashvale, the bestest nosh north o' the Equator. There's a' manner o' things on the menu, but we twa only ever have haddock, chips and peas. It's the nicht oot tae round aff the best day oot. They have a thing on the menu called "The Ashvale Whale". The biggest fish in the sea. It comes wi' chips and peas tae and if you can eat the hale lot, ye get anither ane free. Paw said that once Daphne ate twa and wondered if there was anythin' for efters. But then again, she would.

Ah kent you twins were up tae somethin' fishy!

Highland Games

BRAEMAR GATHERING
by Maggie Broon

And while ye're on Deeside, ye jist must visit <u>BRAEMAR</u>, home of the Braemar Highland Games, the Braemar Gathering as it's known. There are Highland Games all over Scotland, but this is the one Her Majesty attends, so it's the ane a'body remembers. The games are held in The Memorial Park in Braemar. It's been a richt Royal occasion since their new neighbour Queen Victoria attended in 1848 when she'd moved in doon the road. Tickets for The Games sell oot quick . . . and I mean quick. But ye can aye visit at any time and just imagine what it's like . . .the packed crowds, the Queen and her party, the Highland dancing, the pipe bands, Tossing the Caber, Throwing the Hammer and the like and a' thae big lovely young men in skirts . . . sorry, kilts.

But, if ye're no' lucky enough tae get tickets for the Braemar Bash, look out for the hundreds of Highland Games all over Scotland. It really does make a grand day oot.

26   The Sunday Post

Out & About:
The Braemar Gathering

THERE HAVE been gatherings at Braemar for over 900 years. The current form of the Gathering can be traced back to 1832 when the Braemar Highland Society donated money for the prizes and took on the organisation of the Gathering.

The Gathering is held on the first Saturday in September in the Memorial Park in Braemar. It's been a Royal occasion since Queen Victoria first attended in 1848.

Among the events held at the Gathering are:
- Tossing the Caber
- Throwing the Hammer
- Putting the Stone
- The Hill Race,
- The Inter-Services Tug of War
- Highland Dancing competitions
- Pipe Bands

. . . and even the Children's Sack Race.

Looks like he's goin tae drap it

(i) Braemar Gathering
AB35 5YU.
Tel: 013397 41098
www.braemargathering.org

114

THE STONE TOSS

THE STONE TOSS

THE STONE TOSS

116

Pitlochry and the Centre of Scotland

by Daphne Broon

I like PITLOCHRY. The locals tell me it's the very centre of Scotland. It's but a wee stroll fae the railway station tae the Pitlochry dam on Loch Faskally, wi' an ice cream shop on yer way. The big dam is part o' the Hydro scheme built aroond here efter the Second World war. Haudin' back the waters o' bonnie Loch Faskally, Pitlochry dam is a fair lump o' concrete and it has a fish ladder tae help the salmon climb up intae the waters o' the loch. There's an observation room where ye can stick yer nose up against the glass and come face tae face wi' some o' Scotland's best salmon. It's as weel salmon tastes better than it looks. Some o' thae monsters look like something oot o' a scarey movie. And jist a stroll doon river fae the dam is the Pitlochry Festival Theatre. There's something for a' tastes here throughout the year – comedy, folk music, serious plays and near onythin' else ye can think o', includin' salmon in the restaurant.

We dropped the menfolk aff at BLAIR CASTLE jist up the road. It looks fantastic and the lads had a rare afternoon. The castle is the home o' the Dukes o' Atholl and still has its own private army, the only ane in Scotland, apart from The Tartan Army fitba' lot, of course. Blair Castle is a magnificent white building ye can see for miles, and a walk through the grounds wi' the huge trees is awesome.

But for us weemin, it was foot doon on the accelerator and up the road tae the HOUSE OF BRUAR!! It's aboot nine miles fae Pitlochry and is ane o' the best shoppin' days oot in the world. There's a'thing in the shops here fae a coffee an' a scone tae the finest tweeds and woollens the Scottish sheep can produce. Funny how ye can get sic lovely claithes fae thae smelly stupid animals! Ye'll love the braw claithes, the best o' Scottish food and near a'thing else tae warm a lassie's heart and melt her credit card. Dae ye no' jist LOVE shoppin'?

The falls of Bruar. Tranquillity!

(i) Information about Pitlochry
www.pitlochry.org
Pitlochry Festival Theatre PH16 5DR.
Tel: 01796 484626
www.pitlochry.org.uk

(i) Blair Castle PH18 5TL.
Tel: 01796 481207
www.blair-castle.co.uk
House of Bruar PH18 5TZ.
Tel: 01796 483236
www.houseofbruar.com

Pitlochry and the Centre of Scotland

The Sunday Post   32

Moulin Inn & Brewery PH16 5EH.
Tel: 01796 472196
www.moulininn.co.uk
Killiecrankie Visitor Centre
PH16 5LG. Tel: 0844 493 2194
www.nts.org.uk

Beautiful Faskally.

Days Out: Good Walks

THERE ARE many well marked paths in and around Pitlochry, round the loch and through the woods at Faskally. If you are on the round-the-loch walk, stop at the boat station on the water's edge for another ice cream and feed the ducks. For climbers and hill-walkers, a favourite route is up and down Ben Vrackie (2,757 ft). Again, there are well marked paths. Stop and start at the Moulin Inn, where there's a small brewery making its own beer, just about essential after coming down off the hill.

THE PASS OF KILLIECRANKIE

This is the site of a famous battle on 27 July 1689 between the Jacobites under "Bonnie Dundee" (John Graham of Claverhouse, Viscount Dundee) and King William's troops under General Hugh MacKay. The Jacobites won a convincing victory. There's a famous spot over by the River Garry, called the Soldier's Leap, near the Killiecrankie Visitor Centre. A government soldier, Donald McBean, was being chased at the battle by a Highlander with a great sword and didn't fancy his chances, so he leapt right across the rocks over the torrent. It's an Olympic leap, as you'll see, of around 18½ ft. "Bonnie Dundee" was not so lucky, for he was killed when leading the Highlanders in a charge and lies buried in the nearby graveyard at Old Blair.

The dam and fish ladder.

119

Great Gardens

Maw really likes visitin' beautiful gardens, perhaps cos we dinnae have a garden at Glebe Street. The rest o' us enjoy seeing the ootside tamed. Here are some o' the best.

Pitmedden Garden

PITMEDDEN GARDEN is 1 mile west of Pitmedden village and 14 miles north of Aberdeen. It's hard to imagine a garden today being planted on such an extravagant scale. The heart of the property is the formal walled garden originally laid out in 1675 by Sir Alexander Seton. Today, Pitmedden features over 5 miles of box hedging arranged in intricate patterns to form six parterres. Each parterre is filled with some 40,000 plants bursting with colour in the summer months. The adjoining Museum of Farming Life brings the agricultural past to life.

Out & About: *Gardens*

Threave Garden

THREAVE GARDEN, 1 mile west of Castle Douglas, is best known for its magnificent display of nearly 200 different varieties of springtime daffodils, but this is very much a garden for all seasons. Highlights of the 64-acre garden are the rose garden, the impressive walled garden and stunning herbaceous borders. The principal rooms of the Scottish Baronial-style Threave House are now open to visitors.

The Countryside Centre features interactive displays and a live video link to one of the many nesting boxes on the wider estate, with its waymarked trails, bird hides, and wildfowl sanctuary.

Inverewe Garden IV22 2LG.
Tel: 0844 493 2225
Threave Garden DG7 1RX.
Tel: 0844 493 2245
Greenbank Garden G76 8RB.
Tel: 0844 493 2201
Pitmedden Garden AB41 7PD
Tel: 0844 493 2177
Details for all four gardens above at www.nts.org.uk

Drummond Gardens

Drummond is near Muthill and south of Crieff in Perthshire. If you have seen the film "Rob Roy" you will have seen these gardens, for they are where Montrose held court. The main garden, sitting below Drummond Castle, is laid out in the formal style of the 17th century, with the overall shape of the design based on the Saltire. There is a strong north–south axis to the garden, starting with the wide flight of steps down from the castle to the 17th century sundial in the centre of the garden. This line then continues through a stone arch and the kitchen garden, and then rises through the trees to the top of the hillside opposite the castle. It is an amazing sight.

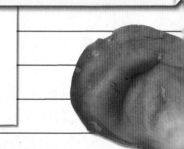

Out & About: *Gardens*

LOGAN BOTANIC GARDEN

Logan Garden, about 14 miles south of Stranraer, is an exotic paradise tucked away on the south-western tip of the country. Warmed by the Gulf Stream, the Walled Garden is breathtaking. From spring to late autumn, a blaze of colour greets the eye and the air is heavy with exotic scents. With a backdrop of palms and tree ferns, the atmosphere on a sunny day is truly tropical. The Woodland Garden has a host of weird and wonderful plants and trees such as the gunnera bog. It is a regional garden of the Royal Botanic Garden, Edinburgh.

The Scots Magazine   63

Great Scottish Gardens

Inverewe Garden

One of the world's greatest gardens, Inverewe, 6 miles north-east of Gairloch, sprang from one man's determination and his taste for the exotic. This 50-acre garden was created by Osgood Mackenzie in 1862. For many, visiting this beautiful, tranquil place is an unforgettable experience. The garden is built on a craggy hillside with a majestic setting on the edge of Loch Ewe.

It is an oasis of exotic plants, bursting with vibrant colour – thanks to the warm currents of the Gulf Stream that flow along the west Scottish coastline. Rhododendrons from the Himalayas, eucalypts from Tasmania, Olearia from New Zealand, and other species from such far-flung places as Chile and South Africa all flourish here, in a display that changes with the seasons, so repeat visits are always rewarded. The Walled Garden looks its best in spring through to late summer when flowering bulbs and plants are grown alongside vegetables which traditionally were for the "family" in the "Big Hoose".

Greenbank Garden

Greenbank Garden is in Clarkston, about 6 miles south of the centre of Glasgow. It is a unique walled garden of 2.5 acres with plants and designs of special interest to gardeners. There are 447 varieties of daffodils and more than 3,700 different plants in the garden. The walled garden is surrounded by 15 acres of woodland walks. The garden is used to assess what plants are suitable for a Scottish climate. Greenbank House was built in the 1760s and is sometimes open to the public at the weekends.

(i)

Drummond Gardens PH5 2AA.
Tel: 01764 681433
www.drummondcastlegardens.co.uk
Logan Botanic Garden DG9 9ND.
Tel: 01776 860231
www.rbge.org.uk/the-gardens/logan

Dundee

THE CITY OF DISCOVERY
by Joe Broon

It's on the very banks o' the <u>Silvery Tay</u>, the mightiest river in Scotland, that yer day oot in <u>DUNDEE</u> starts.

Get aff the train at Dundee Station and then ye canna miss the <u>RRS DISCOVERY</u>. It's Dundee's most famous ship, built tae transport Captain Scott tae the Antarctic over a hundred years ago in 1901. Dundee was a famous whaling city and the Discovery was built here. Ye can tour the ship and its museum at <u>DISCOVERY QUAY</u>. Marvel at the ship's huge timbers, able tae withstand the Antarctic ice pack (and a guid job, too, as the ship was frozen in the ice for two years) and at the cramped quarters the crew shared below decks. Also berthed in Dundee is <u>HM FRIGATE UNICORN</u>, one of the last of the Royal Navy's wooden ships, launched in 1824.

Then there's the <u>VERDANT WORKS</u>, tellin' the story of ane o' Dundee's famous "Three Js" . . . Jute, Jam and Journalism. It is an old jute works and the shake, rattle an' roar o' the original machinery will transport ye back a hunner years tae when jute was King and Dundee was its capital city. The museum is just the most fascinating look back intae a time when 50,000 folk were employed in the jute trade in Dundee.

In the city centre pedestrian area is the best-known cowboy in Scotland. Cast in bronze, the statue o' Desperate Dan mingles wi' the shoppers as he strides across the foot o' Reform Street. He's Dan fae <u>The Dandy</u>, one of Dundee's two famous children's comics. Sneaking up behind him is another showbiz star, Minnie the Minx from <u>The Beano</u> comic, with her catapult aimed at Dan's back. Kids love getting their photies taken beside the two giants from Dundee.

by The Twins
Oor favourite place in Dundee is the <u>SENSATION SCIENCE CENTRE</u>. We're no' very keen on science at school, but this is different. It's supposed tae be for kids, but Granpaw and Paw liked it as much as we did. And it's in the Greenmarket, jist twa minutes' walk from the train. We hate trailing aboot and that's what we like aboot Dundee. Lots o' the things ye want tae see are near the station.

(i) Dundee Women's Trail celebrates twenty-five amazing women whose lives touched the city. There is a map to follow to take a walk in some great women's shoes. You can download and print a map or a copy of the Dundee Women's Trail information leaflet to take with you.
www.dundeewomenstrail.org.uk

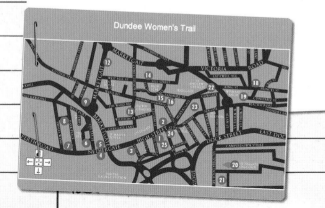

RRS Discovery, DD1 4XA.
Tel: 01382 309060
www.rrsdiscovery.com
Verdant Works, DD1 5BT.
Tel: 01382 309060
www.rrsdiscovery.com

Dundee
CITY OF DISCOVERY......

BROUGHTY FER

TAYPAR

A Beautiful House
looking the River
large rooms, Sun
Adequate staff,
for
Gol

MOD
arage
R. C

ty F

RRS Dis

Days Out: Two walks in Dundee

Walk No. 1 takes you along the river front at the railway station away from the city centre. You'll easily see what's ahead of you – the famous Tay Railway Bridge. It was once the longest in the world. The original bridge fell down in 1879 and you can see the "feet" of the old bridge sticking out of the water alongside the "new" bridge, as well as seals lying on the sand banks after eating salmon for their lunch. When you're up close to the bridge, it's a marvellous sight, with the big express trains rattling over your head.

Walk No. 2 takes you to the summit of Dundee Law, the hill that overlooks the city. There's an indicator on the top of the hill pointing out the things you can see in all directions, from the River Tay and the bridges at your feet to the high hills of Perthshire. It's worth the effort and it will give you an appetite for the world-famous Dundee peh (that's Dundonian for "pie") or an ingin (onion) bridie.

Desperate Dan - Dundee City Square

HM Frigate Unicorn,
DD1 3JA. Tel: 01382 200900
www.frigateunicorn.org
Sensation, DD1 4QB.
Tel: 01382 228800
www.sensation.org.uk
Dundee information:
www.angusanddundee.co.uk

Abbeys tae Visit

Abbeys are places where monks used tae live, work an' pray. They were built hunners o' years ago and nearly all o' them are now ruins. I did a project on ane famous abbey — Arbroath Abbey. It's famous because o' the Declaration o' Arbroath, which is nothin' to do wi' Arbroath Smokies, but that's just one o' the reasons we like comin' here.

Arbroath Abbey

Arbroath Abbey was founded in 1178 by King William I 'the Lion' as a memorial to his friend Thomas Becket, Archbishop of Canterbury, who was murdered in 1170. William asked the monks from Kelso Abbey to start the monastery. When he died in 1214, his body was buried in front of the high altar. Traditionally, Scottish Kings were laid to rest at Dunfermline Abbey.

There are some buildings grouped to the south side of the church and another group further south. All that's left of these are foundations, but if you shut your eyes tight, you can imagine just what it was like. They say that the abbot's house is one of the most complete abbot's residences left in the whole country. Nearby are the gatehouse, the guesthouse and a long stretch of the outer wall. There's plenty of space for a picnic and room for the Bairn and the Twins to run about.

The Declaration of Arbroath is the most famous document in Scottish history. When Robert the Bruce beat Edward II of England at Bannockburn in 1314, this did not end the Wars of Independence. The English persuaded Pope John XXII to retain the sentence of excommunication passed on King Robert in 1306. In response, 40 Scottish nobles, barons and freemen despatched a note to Pope John. This letter set out Scotland's case that it was an independent kingdom. It was written down by Abbot Bernard of Arbroath, King Robert's chancellor, and was sent from here in April 1320.

The guidebook says that religious life in the abbey continued until the Scottish Reformation in 1560. In 1580 parts of the abbey were dismantled to build a new burgh church. By 1700 the buildings were in much the same condition they are now. The abbey's famous 'Round O' – the circular window in the south transept gable – became a landmark for shipping. Robert Stevenson, grandfather of the novelist Robert Louis Stevenson, rebuilt it in 1809.

In March 1951 the abbey was in the papers again, when the Stone of Destiny was found beside the high altar, three months after it was pinched back from Westminster Abbey. All quiet since then.

(i) Arbroath Abbey DD11 1EG.
Tel: 01241 878756
Arbroath and the other abbeys listed (apart from Paisley) are looked after by Historic Scotland
www.historic-scotland.gov.uk

Melrose Abbey.

For, as long as but a hundred of us remain alive, never will we on any conditions be brought under English rule. It is in truth not for glory, nor riches, nor honours that we are fighting, but for freedom - for that alone, which no honest man gives up but with life itself.

(from the Declaration of Arbroath)

Paisley Abbey PA1 1JG
Tel: 0141 889 7654
www.paisleyabbey.org.uk

The Scots Magazine   33

Other famous Abbeys

Cambuskenneth Abbey (near Stirling)

Cambuskenneth Abbey was the site of Robert the Bruce's parliament in 1326. James III and his queen are buried here. Today the tower is the only significant remaining section but the majority of the foundations remain.

Crossraguel Abbey (near Maybole, South Ayrshire)

The building of this abbey began in the 13th century. The following three centuries saw the abbey undergo a great deal of rebuilding. Today the remains of the abbey are largely intact, and it is possible to see the church, cloister, chapterhouse, dovecot and living quarters.

Dunfermline Abbey and Palace
(Dunfermline, Fife)

The remains of the 11th-century Benedictine abbey, founded by Queen Margaret, are substantial. Robert the Bruce is buried in the choir. Next to the abbey are the ruins of the royal palace built for James VI, which was the birthplace of Charles I, the last monarch to be born in Scotland.

Inchcolm Abbey (opposite Aberdour, Fife)

Inchcolm island in the Firth of Forth has the best-preserved group of monastic buildings in Scotland, including a 13th-century octagonal chapterhouse. The abbey was founded in 1123.

Jedburgh Abbey (Jedburgh, Scottish Borders)

This great ruin, founded in 1138 by David I, is mostly built in Romanesque and early Gothic styles. The remains include the recently uncovered cloister buildings where several finds were made, including the 12th-century 'Jedburgh comb'.

Kelso Abbey (Kelso, Scottish Borders)

This abbey, which is now in ruins, was founded in 1128 by Benedictine monks from Chartres in France who were brought to Kelso by David I.

Melrose Abbey (Melrose, Scottish Borders)

This is one of the most famous ruins in Scotland. It was founded as a Cistercian abbey in 1136 by David I but was largely destroyed by the English army of Richard III in 1385. The best surviving remains are the church, dating from the 15th century. Robert the Bruce's heart is buried here.

Paisley Abbey (Paisley, Renfrewshire)

The abbey, still used as a church today, was founded in 1163, but much of what you see today dates from the 14th and 15th centuries. There are lots of stained glass windows and its organ is one of the finest in Europe.

EDINBURGH
INTERNATIONAL
FESTIVAL

The Edinburgh Festival
fringe

FESTIVALS

Scotland loves festivals! Loves them? We invented them! Since the time of the first Christian missionaries, when the religion in Scotland was Druidism, a form of sun-worship special to the Celti peoples, Scotland celebrated two festivals a year: Beltane (May 1) and Samhuinn (November 1), which marked the entry of summer and winter. Today the festival of Hallowe'en, on 31 October, still us many folk customs while the original significance has been forgotte So, from Hallowe'en to art, and fire, music and Vikings. While the li below does not include all of Scotland's festivals, many provide all-round family entertainment. It's time to have a day oot, and celebr

Hebridean Celtic Festival
www.hebceltfest.com
Up-Helly-Aa, Shetland
www.uphellyaa.org
Aberdeen International Youth Festival
www.aiyf.org
Loch Shiel Spring Festival www.lochshielfestival.com
StAnza Poetry Festival, St Andrews www.stanzapoetry.org
Speyfest www.speyfest.com
Tarbert Music Festival www.auqn74.dsl.pipex.com
Traquair Fair www.traquair.co.uk/fair.html (no fair in 2009)
The WickerMan Festival www.thewickermanfestival.co.uk
Lanark Medieval Festival www.lanarkmedievalfestival.co.uk
Pittenweem Arts Festival www.pittenweemartsfestival.co.uk/
Largs Viking Festival www.largsvikingfestival.com
Wigtown Book Festival www.wigtown-booktown.co.uk
Borders Book Festival www.bordersbookfestival.org
The Word – Aberdeen's Book Festival
www.abdn.ac.uk/word

EDINBURGH
Edinburgh International Festival www.eif.co.uk
Edinburgh Festival Fringe www.edfringe.com
Edinburgh International Book Festival
www.edbookfest.co.uk
Edinburgh International Film Festival
www.edfilmfest.org.uk
Edinburgh Science Festival www.sciencefestival.co.uk
Edinburgh Tattoo www.edintattoo.co.uk
Imaginate Festival (Children's International Theatre Festival)
www.imaginate.org.uk
Edinburgh Harp Festival www.harpfestival.co.uk
Edinburgh's Hogmanay www.edinburghshogmanay.org
Beltane Fire Festival, Edinburgh www.beltane.org

GLASGOW
Celtic Connections www.celticconnections.com
Glasgow Film Festival www.glasgowfilmfestival.org.uk
Merchant City Festival www.merchantcityfestival.com
West End Festival www.westendfestival.co.uk
Aye Write! Glasgow's Book Festival www.ayewrite.com

Oor Favourite Castles

There are lots o' castles tae visit in Scotland. I've mentioned quite a few on other pages. Here are some more great places tae explore. All these castles are looked after by Historic Scotland, and here are some o' the things they say aboot them.

(i)

Bothwell Castle G71 8BL.
Tel: 01698 816894
Huntly AB54 4SH.
Tel: 01466 793191
Castle Campbell FK14 7PP.
Tel: 01259 742408
www.historic-scotland.gov.uk

Out & About: *Bothwell Castle*

BOTHWELL CASTLE is one of the outstanding monuments of medieval Scotland. It owes its origins to Walter of Moray, a northern aristocratic family who acquired Bothwell in 1242. He (or his son William, known as 'the Rich') created the mighty castle in a spectacular display of feudal pride. Not surprisingly, the Morays' great castle figured prominently in the Wars of Independence with England. Siege followed on siege. The most momentous was Edward I's great siege of 1301.

After the wars, Bothwell Castle passed to another powerful noble family, the Black Douglases. They rebuilt it in an impressive form not envisaged by their predecessors. After the Black Douglases were overthrown in 1455, the castle reverted to the Crown, and its later history was relatively uneventful.

Huntly Castle

HUNTLY CASTLE lies in the green heart of the Aberdeenshire countryside. It is a noble ruin in a beautiful setting, remarkable both for the quality of its architecture and for its eventful history. The stately palace that dominates the site is one of Scotland's most impressive medieval buildings. It was constructed around 1450 by the newly ennobled Earl of Huntly. The 4th Earl, George Gordon, 'Cock o' the North', extensively remodelled it in the 1550s.

His grandson, the 6th Earl, greatly embellished it, outside and in, to celebrate his becoming 1st Marquis of Huntly in 1599. It is the 1st Marquis's work that holds the visitor in thrall today: the great inscription high upon the south front, the heraldic fireplaces inside, and most notable of all, the splendid heraldic carving over the main door.

Castle Campbell

Everyone is awestruck by Castle Campbell. The imposing ruin stands in solemn isolation upon a narrow ridge, overlooked by a crescent of the Ochil Hills. Two precipitous ravines hem it on either side, through which thunder the Burn of Care and the Burn of Sorrow. The setting couldn't be more dramatic.

The oldest part of the stone castle was built in the early 15th century. At that time it was called 'Castle Glume'. Around 1465 it passed through marriage to Colin Campbell, 1st Earl of Argyll. In 1489, the earl changed the name to Castle Campbell. And there the Campbells stayed for the next 200 years. Castle Campbell is one of Scotland's best-preserved tower-house castles. The tower house itself served as the family residence. Standing 66 ft high, it dominates the courtyard.

Out & About: *Castles*

Linlithgow

THE MAJESTIC royal palace of the Stewarts at Linlithgow today lies roofless and ruined. Yet the visitor still feels a sense of awe on entering its gates. It was begun by James I in 1424, rising like a phoenix from the flames following a fire that devastated its predecessor. The Stewart queens especially liked its tranquillity and fresh air. But after 1603, when James VI moved the royal court to London following his coronation as James I of England, the palace fell quickly into decline. The end came ignominiously in September 1745, when a fire swept through the ghostly rooms.

It is majestically situated in the centre of Linlithgow, beside 15th-century St Michael's Kirk, and overlooking the peel (park) and loch. The magnificent great hall – despite being roofless - still has the power to impress. In the courtyard is a beautiful three-tiered fountain. There are cellars, staircases and lots of ruined rooms – it is easy to get lost in it!

Historic Scottish Castles:
Hermitage

HERMITAGE, in deepest Liddesdale, is a lonely spot. The feeling of foreboding is heightened by the presence of the awesome castle ruin. It has inspired colourful local legends – of the wicked Lord Soules and of a giant Englishman with impregnable armour who drowned in the nearby Hermitage Water. In truth, though, Hermitage has no need of myths. It has a history of torture, treason – and romantic trysts – sufficient for a host of castles. It has been described as 'the guardhouse of the bloodiest valley in Britain'.

The mighty stone castle rises up from impressive earthworks. The castle was designed not so much for residence as defence, and the interior is just as dour as the outside. Even in the 16th century, Hermitage was adapted to counter the threat posed by gunpowdered artillery, with gunholes punched through its thick walls, and a massive gun defence built outside, to protect the castle's western approach.

Hermitage Castle.

Caerlaverock

Caerlaverock Castle is one of Scotland's great medieval fortresses. For 400 years it stood on the very edge of the kingdom. To the south, across the Solway Firth, lay England. For most of its history, Caerlaverock played an important role in the defence of the realm. Alexander II of Scotland, needing trusted men to secure the Scottish West March, granted the estate to his chamberlain, Sir John de Maccuswell (Maxwell). Sir John built the 'old' castle. Within 50 years, his nephew, Sir Herbert, had moved to a new castle just 650 ft away to the north. There the Maxwell lords remained for the next 400 years.

Caerlaverock's triangular shape is unique among British castles. Why it was built this way is not known. A walk around the castle gives a sense of its strength. The north tower, facing into Scotland, is a mightily impressive twin-towered gatehouse, where the Maxwells had their private suite of rooms.

We could hae a RaRe game o sojers in Thae castles

I'd throw the pair o' ye in the dungeons!

ⓘ

Hermitage TD9 0LU.
Tel: 01387 376222
Linlithgow EH49 7AL.
Tel: 01506 842896
Caerlaverock DG1 4RU.
Tel: 01387 770244
www.historic-scotland.gov.uk

Stirling and Roond About

It's a MIGHTY "Day Oot" withoot a doot.

<u>by Granpaw Broon</u>

<u>STIRLING CASTLE</u>, for my money is a much grander castle than its more popular neebor, Edinburgh Castle. Historic Scotland have done a grand job here. There wid be little point in me tellin' ye a'thing there is tae see here, as it wid fill a hale book on its own. From the newly refurbished Grand Hall tae the on-going re-creation of "<u>The Hunt of the Unicorn</u>", Europe's finest tapestry series, there's nae end o' things tae marvel at. Mak' sure ye walk up tae the castle through the old parts o' Stirling toon and across the drawbridge intae the castle itsel' past the figure o' <u>Robert the Bruce</u>. Ye'll be singin' "<u>Flower o' Scotland</u>" afore ye've even got inside the place. And the view fae the castle ramparts!! Well, come an' see for yersel' and look doon on the plains where armies hacked themselves tae wee bits to decide the fate of Scotland.

Ye canna miss Stirling Castle of course. If ye need directions, ye need tae see yer optician. It's the gigantic stone building sitting richt across the mighty rock in the centre o' the toon. Ye can see it for miles.

Now, if ye've still enough day left o' yer day oot efter seein' the castle, get yer skates on an' get roond tae the <u>WALLACE MONUMENT</u>. That's anither thing ye canna miss unless it's awfy misty. Ye can see it towering up intae the air no' far north o' the castle. Ye canna mistake it for the castle as it's a different shape . . . and, onyway, if ye've jist visited the castle, how would ye mistake it? This is the monument tae oor Scottish hero Sir William Wallace, better known tae some as jist "The Wallace".

And as if a' that wisnae enough history for one day, the <u>BANNOCKBURN</u> Heritage Centre awaits the visit o' every ane o' Jock Tamson's bairns interested in Scottish History. What a result!! What could we not dae wi' a puckle o' thae stalwart seven thoosand lads for oor fitba' and rugby teams the day? And, by the way, ye can still see Stirling Castle fae the battlefield o' Bannockburn.

Wallace Monument FK9 5LF.
Tel: 01786 472140
www.nationalwallacemonument.com

Stirling Castle FK8 1EJ.
Tel: 01786 450000
www.historic-scotland.gov.uk
Bannockburn FK7 0LJ.
Tel: 0844 493 2139
www.nts.org.uk

Days Out: *The Wallace Monument*

THE WALLACE MONUMENT

Film star Mel Gibson played William Wallace in the blockbuster *"Braveheart"* but the monument is to the man himself. The Monument was completed in 1870. It is built on the top of a rocky crag called Abbey Craig and is 220 feet tall. You will need all your puff to climb the 246 steps to the very top, but you can have a rest on floors one, two and three before you reach the top, which is in the shape of a crown.

You will see The Wallace's sword, a double-handed broadsword 5-feet 4-inches long, on the way up. There are also exhibitions about famous Scots and the building of the monument to break up the climb. From the top you can see where William defeated Edward I's English army at the Battle of Stirling Bridge in 1297. After he was defeated at the Battle of Falkirk in 1298, he was betrayed and hanged and cut into bits by his enemies at Smithfield in London.

People were not very nice in his day, and some say The Wallace himself was a bit of a rascal, but he's in every true Scot's heart.

BANNOCKBURN

Although the site of the actual Battle of Bannockburn is disputed by the historians, the Heritage Centre will fill you in on the possibilities. You must stand on the historic site and look at the magnificent statue of King Robert the Bruce of Scotland on his horse.

He won the famous battle here in 1314 over Edward II's English army and "sent them homeward to think again". The battle lasted for two whole days, 23 and 24 June, and the 7,000 Scottish troops routed the 20,000 English troops around the banks of the Bannock Burn. The victory allowed Robert the Bruce to re-establish an independent Scotland.

Falkirk Wheel

FALKIRK WHEEL and SCOTLAND'S CANALS

by Horace Broon

I used tae build fantastic machines wi' my Lego and Meccano sets in the hoose, but nane o' my wildest dreams would have dreamt up anything like the FALKIRK WHEEL. It's a "lift" that hoists canal boats intae the air!! It's like something ye might expect tae see in a science fiction film . . . and all it does is connect two of Scotland's canals, the Forth and Clyde and the Union. The Wheel is hard tae describe and it's best tae go and see it for yersel'. It can lift eight boats or mair fae one canal tae another. They're baith at different heights, no' something that's handy wi' waterways. I read somewhere that the Falkirk Wheel can lift the equivalent weight o' near 100 African elephants, but why onybody would want tae lift 100 elephants when they could jist as easy walk fae one canal tae anither, I have nae idea. There's an amazing view o' the wheel in operation from a sensational viewpoint at the visitor centre and ye can also go on a boat that tak's ye up the Wheel and then on for a wee canal cruise then back doon again.

THE FORTH AND CLYDE CANAL runs fae Glasgow at Bowling to the River Forth, so it connects the west and the east coasts. The Union Canal branches off at the Falkirk Wheel and runs a' the way tae Edinburgh toon. A' the canals in the central belt were once great wattery ribbons o' commerce, wi' boats an' barges carryin' a' manner o' goods an' chattels. But railways and road transport saw the canals near aboot disappear. Efter some grand restoration work costin' millions o' pounds, the waterways now have a new lease o' life. Goodness knows how many empty bottles, auld cars, iron beds and mountains o' a' manner o' junk were pulled oot o' the watter tae mak' way for the new boats. It's mainly pleasure craft nowadays, but I'd no' be surprised tae see the canals used for trade through time.

And there's lots o' walks and bike tracks running alongside the canals. It's richt popular. Check oot the braw new section and the modern lock at PORT DUNDAS in Glasgow.

(i) The Antonine Wall, built by the Romans between the Clyde and the Forth, goes near the Falkirk Wheel. It was made a World Heritage Site in 2008. Visit www.antoninewall.org for details of sites to visit.

Whit a muckle bit o engineerin

continued on
Newtyle

(i)

The Falkirk Wheel FK1 4RS
Tel: 08700 500208
www.thefalkirkwheel.co.uk
For information about all of Scotland's
canals, visit www.scottishcanals.co.uk

Scotland's other great waterways

The Caledonian Canal splits Scotland from Inverness to Fort William, through Loch Ness, Loch Oich and Loch Lochy and all the locks in between. The canal, which stretches for 60 miles, was opened in 1822 and was built to save boats having to go through the Pentland Firth to get to the other side of Scotland. It has 29 locks, the most impressive being a series of eight locks, called Neptune's Staircase, at Banavie, near Fort William. The canal was designed by the Scottish engineer, Thomas Telford. You can hire all manner of pleasure boats and make the trip yourself but it's more than a day trip ... and watch your boat doesn't get hit by the Loch Ness Monster on the way.

The Crinan Canal runs from Ardrishaig on Loch Fyne to Crinan right on the west coast looking over to the Isle of Jura. It's only 9 miles long, but it saves a 130-mile trip around the Mull of Kintyre. It was opened in 1801 and was designed by another Scottish engineer, John Rennie. With 15 locks to open, it is slow-going, taking around 2 hours for a boat to travel the length of the canal. It's fun to cycle alongside this canal and watch the boats slowly making their way from one lock to the next.

Blair Drummond Safari Park

ON SAFARI
with the Broon Twins

We couldna believe it when Paw said he was takin' us and the rest o' the family "On Safari". Just imagine it . . . us, the laddies fae Glebe Street School, headed for Africa or the Amazon or India or wherever it was we were goin'. David Attenborough here we come!

Well, it wisna Africa or any ither place like that we went tae, actually . . . but it WAS absolutely fan-dabby-tastical. In fact it didna tak' long tae get there at all. We just turned off the M9 motorway at junction 10 on tae the A84 and there we were - BLAIR DRUMMOND SAFARI PARK. I'd hardly digested ma breakfast and there we were, and the best o' it was, there were more wild animals there than ye'd EVER meet "on safari" in a month o' Sundays. Ye'll maybe no' believe this, but there's tigers and lions and rhinos and elephants (really, real ones!!) and there's wallabies, ostriches, sea lions, penguins, chimps, giraffes, bears, birds of prey, zebras and . . . and . . . och, I canna remember. There's hunners!! How often can ye say ye've seen a' that on one DAY OOT?? Oor favourites were – ye winna believe this – the meerkats. They're just SO funny.

There's just LOADS tae do there as well as see all the animals. There's a wooden castle ye can climb up. What a view o' the park fae the top . . . and ye can pick oot a' the animals ye've just visited, and then ye can zip back doon tae the ground on slides. AND there's a big ASTRAGLIDE slide. That's what kids like us like. We couldna keep Granpaw off it!! Oh, and the pedalo-thingy boats that seat four or five folk and ye can sail roond the wee loch. Mak' sure ye only let folk that are prepared tae pedal on yer boat. Daphne just wanted tae lie back an' get suntanned.

Oh . . . nearly forgot. If ye have a wee sister (and we do), make sure she visits the PETS FARM. Ye get tae stroke all the animals that like gettin' tickled – llamas, goats, piggies, sheep an' the like. The Bairn was howlin' when we left. She just didna want tae go hame. Neither did we.

Mother and baby wallaby.

Dinner time for the lions.

LiST o' Things Tae Tak oh SafaRi

piTh helmeTS
heTS Tae caTch shakes ah'
beasTies
a blUnderblIss Tae Ward off
Wild animals
TehTS
binoclLaRs
animal cages
food

(i)

Blair Drummond Safari Park
FK9 4UR. Tel: 01786 841456
www.blairdrummond.com
(closed November to March)

hoRace.
he heVeR
FoRgeTS
anYThin

The East Neuk

The SCOTTISH FISHERIES MUSEUM
by Hen Broon

Situated richt on the harbour front in <u>ANSTRUTHER</u>, the Fisheries Museum is a gem. It's actually worthwhile tae hae a day oot aboot here just tae visit the wee toons and harbours all along the East Neuk o' Fife. But ye'd be missin' a treat no' tae spend time in this history of Scottish fisher-folk and their hard-won sea harvest.

The museum itself is a fascinatin' collection of historic hooses an' cottages in the heart of the village. I first went there wi' Paw and Joe when it opened in 1969. We'd been fishin' oorsels that day, withoot much luck I hasten tae add. The museum's jist got bigger and bigger since then, a bit like the fish Paw caught that day gets bigger an' bigger wi' the story-tellin'.

Ye'll find there's something here for a' the femily. The museum is "broken up" into a range of galleries, makin' it easy tae find what ye want. There are literally tens of thousands of things tae see, from paintings and auld photographs tae a whole collection of actual historic boats. There's a big ane ca'd "Zulu" that's 78 ft long. Find oot aboot how yer Anstruther ancestors actually caught fish. Marvel at the photies of "the silver darlings". . . no' the bonnie fisher-lassies fae the local dances, but the name given by folk tae the millions o' herring that once used tae be landed. There's naturally a memorial room to remind ye o' the "real price of fish", the hundreds of brave fisher-folk who have lost their lives in the dangerous waters around the Scottish coast.

While ye're there, what better way tae finish aff a day at the fishing museum then a visit tae the finest fish and chip shop in the country. And that's Official (or is that OFISHAL?). It's the Anstruther Fish Bar, UK winner of Seafish Fish & Chip Shop of the Year 2008/2009. It's been winning awards for years and a fish supper there will tell ye why. And it's only a stone's throw fae the museum richt on the harbour front. Sit in an' eat or take an' oot on yer day oot an' sit at the harbour's edge.

So there ye go, sling yer hook an' get doon tae the Neuk!!

(i)

Scottish Fisheries Museum
KY10 3AB. Tel: 01333 310628
www.scotfishmuseum.org
Anstruther Fish Bar KY10 3AQ.
Tel: 01333 310518
www.anstrutherfishbar.co.uk

Falkland Palace

THE PALACE is in the town of Falkland in Fife, nestling at the foot of the Lomond Hills. Built by James IV and James V between 1450 and 1541, it was a country retreat of the Stuart monarchs of Scotland for over 200 years and much enjoyed by Mary, Queen of Scots.

Entering the Palace through the Gatehouse, visitors come to the courtyard, enclosed on two sides by the South Range and the now ruined East Range, accidentally destroyed in 1654 when Cromwell's troops were garrisoned at the Palace, which originally housed the Royal Apartments. The architecture of the building and restoration works carried out by the 3rd Marquis of Bute in the 19th century can be easily examined from here.

The Gatehouse, completed in 1541, contains the private quarters of the Keepers of Falkland Palace, a hereditary position of which the present holder is Ninian Crichton Stuart of Falkland.

The Chapel Royal is the most significant surviving original interior of the Palace and dates from the reign of James V. The oak entrance screen and painted ceiling are of national importance and a set of 17th century Flemish tapestries tell the story of Joseph and Benjamin. The

Tapestry Gallery forms the processional route from the King's Apartments to the Chapel Royal. The gallery is hung with 17th century "Verdure" tapestries. Look out for the goat with the eyes that follow you as you walk by!

Gardens

The orchard is in its original 17th-century site and contains a large selection of fruit trees, including apple, pear, plum and cherry. The herbaceous borders in the main garden provide a colourful setting for the Palace.

Falkland Palace
KY15 7BU.
Tel: 0844 493 2186
www.nts.org.uk

Anstruther.

When was the sky ever this blue
on oor day oot?

St Andrews

ⓘ St Andrews Links Trust ...
9XL. Tel: 01334 46666...
www.standrews.org.uk
Secret Bunker KY16 8QH...
Tel: 01333 310301 www...
secretbunker.co.uk
St Andrews information:
www.saint-andrews.co...
www.visit-standrews.co...

SECRET BUN...
Scotland's
Best Kept Sec...
www.secretbunker.c...

Sections 10 & 11 15

from the Links. 9...

The Sunday Post 28

Days Out: *Scotland's Secret Bunker*

Just 7 miles outside St Andrews you can find Scotland's best kept secret. At ground level it looks just like any other farmhouse, but 100 feet under the ground beneath it is hidden an enormous former government control centre. It consists of two floors, each the size of a football pitch. If there had been a nuclear war, this is where Scotland would have been governed from.

The Bunker contained everything that was needed to survive a nuclear attack. Around 300 people could live there, protected by 15-ft thick concrete walls and a 3-ton door, and it even had its own cinema.

It was built in the 1950s and nobody knew it was there. You can now explore the Bunker and discover what it was like to live with the threat of nuclear war.

It's a visit you will not forget – and make sure you don't get trapped in at closing time . . . The Secret Bunker is open from March to the end of October and it is now well sign-posted so that you can find it.

...RET ...UNKER
...Scottish Farmhou...
...land's Secret Bur...
...ft accommodatio...
...ight world of the ...
...d War. Take the ...
...er how they would...
...er you wouldn't !!!...
...est & Best Kept Sec...

ⓘ St Andrews Castle KY16 9AR.
Tel: 01334 477196
www.historic-scotland.gov.uk
St Andrews Cathedral KY16 9QL.
Tel: 01334 472563
www.historic-scotland.gov.uk
St Andrews Aquarium
KY16 9AS. Tel: 01334 474786
www.standrewsaquarium.co.uk

POST CARD
CORRESPONDENCE   Printed in Gt. Britain

Havin' a great
week here in
St Andrews. Hen
got a new record
at the old course.
He took a 17 at
the 17th.

    Joe xx

The Broon Family
Glebe Street
Scotland
UK

ST. ANDREWS
4 9PM
14 JLY
1959
FIFE

3d

ST ANDREWS
by Maw Broon hersel'

ST ANDREWS, the home of GOLF, or so they tell me. It's ane o' my favourite places and it's like nae place else in Scotland. Sadly there's nae railway station here, and if ye dinna come in yer ain car, ye need either tae get a bus or get the train tae Leuchars Station and catch the local bus.

Ye jist canna come tae St Andrews and no' see the world-famous golf course, but me I stick tae the putting greens. And what's mair, if ye do want tae play, ye'll need mair than a few bawbees for yer round. That's what happens when ye have the maist famous golf course in the world richt in the toon. But it is worth a look-see.

Whatever else ye dae, dinna miss the impressive CASTLE and visitor centre (ye'll kick yersel' if ye miss this). Dinna drop intae the bottle-nose dungeon, mind, cos it's impossible tae get oot. And then there's the ruined CATHEDRAL. The teeth o' the ruins jist soar up intae the sky. It must have been some place afore it was knocked aboot a bit. Goodness knows what the heating bills must hae been like. But it's lovely tae sit there in the gardens wi' a nice flask o' tea and a sandwich an' let yer mind wander.

There's TWA beaches at St Andrews, the East and the West Sands. Now there's the perfect spot tae unwind an' let yer bairns run aboot efter a visit tae a' the wee shops. And St Andrews has some lovely wee shops . . . golf shops, woollen shops, gift shops, whisky shops (Granpaw and Paw were in there near a' day), a lovely cheese shop and ane selling the best ice cream ye've ever tasted.

If ye're in the toon in early August dinna miss the Lammas Fair and in April there is the Kate Kennedy Procession . . . and there's the ST ANDREWS AQUARIUM that yer bairns will love, richt on the sea shore.

So, jist a wee taster of what's tae see oot there on the east coast. An' ye dinna hae tae be handicapped trauchlin' a' that golf equipment aboot tae hae a real day oot in this historic stone toon.

US

West Sands - St Andrews

THE EASTERN

37548 38B

NOT TRANSFERABLE

SINGLE

139

On The Beach

WE DO LIKE TAE BE BESIDE THE SEASIDE
by Maw Broon

The Broon family DO like tae be beside the sea. For me, it's a great day oot and I can lie back an' read a book while a'body does their different things. The Bairn will sit for hours makin' castles wi' the Twins, Horace rakes aboot in pools for sea creatures, Granpaw and Paw sit wi' their coolbox and occasionally roll up their trooser legs and hae a paddle (I suspect Granpaw, the auld rogue, does this mair often when there's a bonnie lassie aboot). Hen an' Joe, like a' big bairns, like horsin' aboot in the waves and Maggie and Daphne jist sit lookin' bonnie an' fryin' themselves in sun oil.

Now, there's a' manner o' whit folk are callin' AWARD beaches – there's Blue Flag beaches, Yellow Flag beaches – and they're the places tae look oot for. The sand is clean and the water is safe for bathin'. There were only 6 o' the best Blue Flag beaches in Scotland in 2008 and maist o' them were on the East coast, which was a surprise tae me, as I've been on many bonnie bonnie stretches o' sand up and doon the West for years. No' that I dinna like the winners on the East ye ken, Aberdour, St Andrews an' the like. Ye'll find a list o' thae spots under SEASIDE AWARDS or whatever on yer computer (even we have ane now).

So, Yellow or Blue, ye pays yer money an' takes yer choice. Here's the top six BROON FLAG beaches dotted up an' doon the West coast that mak' a great "day oot". Sorry if I've no' listed yer favourite.

ⓘ

Seaside Award Beaches
in Scotland
www.keepscotlandbeautiful.org/
index.asp?pg=3

The Broon flag beaches

1) **Islay. Laggan Beach**, not far from the ferry port at Port Ellen, stretches for miles and miles nearly all the way to Bowmore. There's birds of all shapes and sizes swooping about and with the waves making music on the sand, it's heaven. Start at a wee place called Kintra in the big sand dunes. (Another Islay favourite is Machir Bay. It's breathtaking.)

2) **Calgary Beach, Isle of Mull**. About 11 miles from Tobermory, an absolute must.

3) **Sanna Sands**. It's at the west end of the Ardnamurchan peninsula. Stand at the water's edge and just look out into the Minch.

4) **Sandaig Bay**, near Glenelg. This is where Gavin Maxwell wrote the book about the otters, *The Ring of Bright Water*. There's a memorial to one of his pet otters, Edal. Even though it's called Sandaig, it's not very sandy, but it's a wonderful spot. There's a short walk down from the road, but it's worth the effort.

5) **Achmelvich Bay**, north of Lochinver. Stunningly beautiful. Watch the setting sun turn the Sutherland mountains pink. You will feel proud to be Scottish.

6) **Sandwood Bay**. In the far North West, on the road to Durness, turn off to Kinlochbervie and follow the coast road until you reach the car park. Sandwood Bay is then a few miles walk. You should take a map, but the walk is not difficult. It is wild and not for swimming, but it's one of the most beautiful bays in the world. Watch the big booming breakers hammer down on the sands. Magic.

Horace's Really Useful Index

Note: there are references to Historic Scotland and the National Trust for Scotland throughout the book. For more details on these organisations see pages 2-3.

abbeys 124-5
Abbotsford House 27
Aberdeen 53, 112-13
Aberdeen Art Gallery
    and Museum 56
Aberdeen Maritime Museum 28
Achmelvich Bay, Lochinver 141
Anstruther 136-7
Arbroath Abbey 124
Arisaig 83
Armadale 84
Arran 38-41
Art Galleries 56
Arthur's Seat 14
Ashvale Fish Restaurant,
    Aberdeen 113
Auchindrain Museum 64
Aviemore 100
Ayrshire 32-3
Ballachulish 75
Balmoral Castle 110-11
Bannockburn 130, 131
Bass Rock 25
Baxter's Highland Village,
    Fochabers 92
Beaches 140-41
Ben Nevis 76-9
birds, where to see them 94-5
Blackhouse, Arnol, Lewis 97
Blair Castle 117
Blair Drummond Safari Park
    134-5
Blairquhan 33
Bonawe Ironworks 66
Borders, The 26-7
Botanic Gardens 52-3
Bothwell Castle 127
Braemar Gathering 114-15
Broadford 85
Brodick Castle 41
Broughton House 31
Buachaille Etive Mor 74
Burns National Heritage Park 36
Burns, Robert 30, 31, 36-7
Burrell Collection,
    Glasgow 51, 56
Caerlaverock 30, 128
Cairngorm Mountain funicular
    100, 101
Cairngorm Reindeer herd 104

Cairngorms, The 100-01
Calanais, Lewis 97
Caledonian Canal 88, 133
Caledonian MacBrayne 68, 70,
    72-73, 84-5, 108
Calgary beach, Mull 68, 141
Calton Hill, Edinburgh 18
Cambuskenneth Abbey 125
camping 102
Castle Campbell 127
castles 127-9
Codona's Amusement Park,
    Aberdeen 112
country parks 58-9
Craignure 68
Cream o'Galloway Visitor
Centre 30
Creetown Gem Rock
    Museum 28
Crianlarich 81
Crinan Canal 65, 88, 133
Crossaguel Abbey 33, 125
Cruachan 66
Cuillins 87
Culbin Sands, Nairn 95
Culloden Battlefield 92, 93
Culzean Castle 34
Dallas Dhu Distillery 106
Dean Castle 33
Deep Sea World, North
    Queensferry 20
Deeside 110-11, 114-5,
Denny Tank, Dumbarton 28
Dirleton Castle 25
Discovery Quay, Dundee 122
distilleries, whisky 106-9
Drummond Gardens 120
Drumnadrochit 88, 90
Dryburgh Abbey 27
Duart Castle 68
Dumfries and Galloway 30-31
Dundee 122-23
Dundee Botanic Gardens 53
Dundee Contemporary Arts 56
Dundrennan 31, 124-5
Dunfermline Abbey 125
Dunfermline Abbot House
    Heritage Centre 28
Dunollie Castle 67
Dunvegan Castle 86
Duthie Park and Winter Garden,
    Aberdeen 53
Dynamic Earth, Edinburgh 28
East Lothian 24-5
Edinburgh 8-18
Edinburgh Castle 8-9
Edinburgh City of Lit. 16

Edinburgh Military Tattoo 8
Edinburgh Zoo 16, 105
Eildon Hills 27
Electric Brae, The 33
Ellisland Farm (Burns) 30
Fairy Glen, Fortrose 95
Falkirk Wheel 132-3
Falkland Palace 137
Falls of Clyde Visitor Centre 44
festivals 126
Fingal's Cave 71
Firth of Forth 19-21
Flodden Field 27
Forestry Commission 58
Fort Augustus 88
Fort George 93
Fort William 76, 79, 82-3, 133
Forth and Clyde Canal 132
Forth Rail Bridge 19-21
Gallery of Modern Art,
    Glasgow 56
Galloway Forest Park 30
Gardens 52-3, 120-21
Georgian House, The 18
Glasgow 48-51, 52, 54-5
Glasgow Botanic Gardens 52
Glasgow Cathedral 51
Glasgow School of Art 54, 55
Glasgow Science Centre 51
Glencoe 74-5
Glenelg 84
Glenfinnan 82
Glenmore 100
Goatfell, Arran 41
Greenbank Garden 121
Gretna Green 31
Grey Mare's Tail waterfall 62
Greyfriar's Bobby 10
Helensburgh 80
Hermitage Castle 128
Hermitage, Dunkeld 62
Highland Wildlife Park 105
Hill House, Helensburgh 55, 80
Holyrood Park 12
Holyroodhouse, Palace of 14-15
House of Bruar 117
Hunterian Art Gallery,
    Glasgow 55, 56
Hunterian Museum, Glasgow 28
Huntly Castle 127
Inchcolm Abbey 125
Inveraray 64-5
Inverewe Garden 121
Iona 70-71
Islands, The 72-3
Islay 108
Jarlshof 99

Jedburgh Abbey 125
John Knox's House 12
John Muir Trust 58
Kelburn Castle 33
Kelso Abbey 125
Kelvingrove Art Gallery
  and Museum 48-9
Kerrera 67
Kilchurn Castle 66
Killiecrankie Visitor Centre 118
Kilmartin Glen, Argyll 97
Kinlochleven 74
Kirkcaldy Museum and
  Art Gallery 56
Kirkcudbright 31
Kyleakin 84
Kylerhea 84
Laggan beach, Islay 141
Largs, Battle of 99
Lerwick 99
Linlithgow Castle 128
Loch Awe 66
Loch Faskally 117
Loch Garten, Aviemore 95, 104
Loch Gruinart, Islay 95
Loch Lomond 60-61, 81
Loch Long 81
Loch Morlich 100
Loch Ness 88-9
Loch Ness Monster, and
  Daphne 89
Loch Nevis 94
Lochalsh 84
Lochnagar 110
Lochranza Distillery
  Visitor Centre 38
Lochwinnoch 95
Logan Botanic Garden 121
Lost Valley, Glencoe 75
Luss 61
Machir Bay, Islay 141
Machrie Standing Stones,
  Arran 39
Mackintosh, Charles Rennie
  54-5
Maid of the Loch 61
Mallaig 83, 94
Melrose Abbey 125
Mull, Isle of 68-9, 73
Museum of Childhood,
  Edinburgh 12
Museum of Scottish Lighthouses,
  Fraserburgh 28
Museum of Transport,
  Glasgow 51
Museums 28
Nardini's, Largs 99

National Gallery of Scotland 18
National Museum of
  Costume 31
National Museum of Flight 24
National Museum of
  Rural Life 46
National Museum of
  Scotland 18
National War Memorial 9
New Lanark 44
Oban 67, 68
One o'Clock Gun 8
Ossian's Hall waterfall 62
Paisley Abbey 125
People's Palace, Glasgow 51
Perth Museum and Art
  Gallery 56
Pier Arts Centre, Stromness 56
Pitlochry 117-18
Pitmedden Garden 120
Port Dundas 132
Preston Mill 44
Queen's Cross Church,
  Glasgow 55
Rannoch 81, 82
Robert Smail's Printing Works,
  Innerleithen 26
Rogie Falls 62
Rosslyn Chapel 16
Rothiemurchus 100, 101
Royal Botanic Gardens,
  Edinburgh 53
Royal Highland Show 22-3
Royal Mile, Edinburgh 10-13
Royal Yacht Britannia 16
RSPB 58, 94
Sandaig Bay, Glenelg 141
Sandwood Bay, near
  Durness 141
Sanna Sands, Ardnamurchan
  141
Scotland Street School,
  Glasgow 55
Scott Monument 18
Scottish Fisheries Museum 136
Scottish Maritime Museum,
  Irvine 32
Scottish Mining Museum 24
Scottish National Gallery of
  Modern Art 56
Scottish Natural Heritage 58
Scottish Parliament 14, 15
Scottish Seabird Centre 25
Scottish Sealife Sanctuary 67
Scottish Storytelling Centre 12
Seaside Awards 140
Secret Bunker 138

Sensation Science Centre,
  Dundee 122
Skara Brae, Orkney 96
Skye 84-7
Sligachan 85
Smailholm Tower 27
St Andrews 138-9
St Conan's Church, Loch Awe 66
St Giles Cathedral,
  Edinburgh 12
St Mungo Museum of Religious
  Life, Glasgow 51
Staffa 71
Stanley Mills 44
Stirling Castle 130
Stone of Destiny 9, 124
Summerlee Heritage Park 28
Sweetheart Abbey 31
Tam o'Shanter Experience 36
Tantallon Castle 25
Tay Railway Bridge 123
Tenement House, The 50
Threave Garden 120
Tobermory 68, 69
Traquair House 27
Unicorn, Dundee 122
Up-Helly-Aa 98, 99,
Urquhart Castle 88, 90-91
Vane Farm, Kinross 95
Verdant Works, Dundee 122
Very old places 96-7
Vikings, The 98-9
Wallace Monument 130,131
waterfalls 62
Waverley, The 42-3
West Highland Line 80-83
West Highland Way 74, 81
whisky 106-9
Willow Tea Rooms 55
Women's Trail, Dundee 122
Woodland Trust 58
Writers' Museum, Edinburgh 10

The Broons' Days Oot!
Great money-saving offers from
The National Trust for Scotland and Historic Scotland

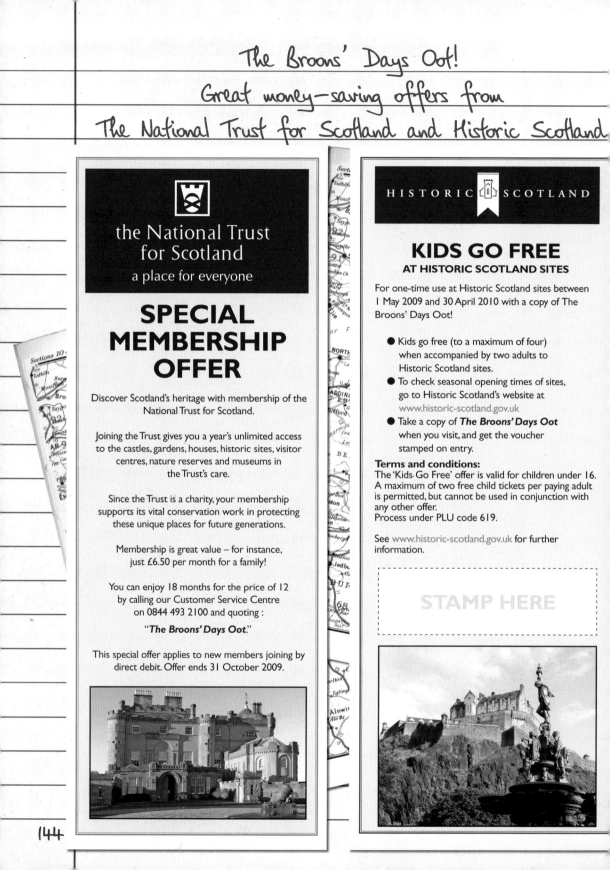

the National Trust for Scotland
a place for everyone

SPECIAL MEMBERSHIP OFFER

Discover Scotland's heritage with membership of the National Trust for Scotland.

Joining the Trust gives you a year's unlimited access to the castles, gardens, houses, historic sites, visitor centres, nature reserves and museums in the Trust's care.

Since the Trust is a charity, your membership supports its vital conservation work in protecting these unique places for future generations.

Membership is great value – for instance, just £6.50 per month for a family!

You can enjoy 18 months for the price of 12 by calling our Customer Service Centre on 0844 493 2100 and quoting :

"The Broons' Days Oot."

This special offer applies to new members joining by direct debit. Offer ends 31 October 2009.

HISTORIC SCOTLAND

KIDS GO FREE
AT HISTORIC SCOTLAND SITES

For one-time use at Historic Scotland sites between 1 May 2009 and 30 April 2010 with a copy of The Broons' Days Oot!

- Kids go free (to a maximum of four) when accompanied by two adults to Historic Scotland sites.
- To check seasonal opening times of sites, go to Historic Scotland's website at www.historic-scotland.gov.uk
- Take a copy of *The Broons' Days Oot* when you visit, and get the voucher stamped on entry.

Terms and conditions:
The 'Kids Go Free' offer is valid for children under 16. A maximum of two free child tickets per paying adult is permitted, but cannot be used in conjunction with any other offer.
Process under PLU code 619.

See www.historic-scotland.gov.uk for further information.

STAMP HERE

144